DREAMS into ACTION

Getting what you want!

DREAMS *into* ACTION

Getting what you want!

Milton Katselas

DOVE
BOOKS

ISBN 0-7871-0493-0

Printed in the United States of America

Dove Books
301 North Cañon Drive
Beverly Hills, CA 90210

Distributed by Penguin USA

Text design by Mark Porro and layout by Carolyn Wendt
Jacket design by Mark Porro
Jacket painting by Milton Katselas

First Printing: March 1996

10 9 8 7 6 5

For Jamie and Dena

TABLE OF CONTENTS

Foreword   xv

Introduction   xvii

Dreams: Real or Fancied?   1

The Flight of a Hawk   6

Career Concept: The Beat of Your Life   10

The Launching Pad   17

Choices   19

The Perfection Syndrome   22

Breaking Down Old Systems   26

Hamal   29

Put Your Ear Up and Let the Guy Talk Into It   40

Free Flowing   49

Getting Along   53

Flinch   57

Terrorist Theater: Getting It Done   65

Celebrate   68

Jewels of the Nile   69

Paint Your Own Portrait   75

Good Moves   77

Levity Sometimes Necessary When
   Talking to Rock   **78**

Horrors!   **84**

Blame Heaven   **86**

Blame: The Cure   **93**

Self-Esteem: What You Deserve   **98**

The Problem Is the Solution   **102**

Scarcity   **108**

Tough Guys   **112**

On Call   **119**

Practicing With Taxi Drivers   **122**

Here Comes Trouble   **126**

Shock Absorbers   **139**

Hitch Up to Your Dream Again   **143**

Certain Down-Home Hints   **145**

Working With Masters   **148**

Give   **153**

Unlikely Winners   **155**

A Freewheeling Discussion   **157**

Career Checklist   **172**

The Dance   **176**

Index   **179**

Change is possible.

Change and the ability to bring about change is what this book is about.

DREAMS into ACTION

Getting what you want!

FOREWORD

You may think you're not an artist. You are. Everyone is, or can be, but it all depends on how you deal with your life. Many approach their lives, their jobs, in an uninvolved, rote fashion. This routine is "fold up your tent and fade away" time.... It's just watching your job and your life slide by. Are you participating or just going through the motions as the clock ticks on? *What* you do is not as vital as *how* you do it. The *how* is taking hold of your job and your life in an exciting, active, and caring way. Actually, there is an art to it. Executives, teachers, custodians, nurses, carpenters, office workers, mechanics, computer programmers, secretaries—all are potential artists and all can become virtuosos. Through years of directing, teaching, and writing I have worked with many artists to help them bring their dreams and careers to resolution. But this desire to fulfill dreams is present in everyone. There are many people walking on the street who, if you talk to them, if you scratch a bit below the surface, will tell you that they have a dream that's not realized.

Someone recently said to me, "I'm afraid to face the challenge of all that I can be." I'd heard that statement before many times. Why? What's holding us back? Why are we afraid? Is it that our full potential might not be enough? Are we afraid to find out? What is it exactly that we want? Will we get it? These questions exist to some degree in all of us. If you don't face the questions, however difficult, and challenge your fears, however stultifying, you will only be able to stand afield, wistfully looking at your dreams, blurry and distant. The answers lie in having the courage to look into ourselves, face our fears, face the truth of what we want, uncover our dreams, and in doing so, bring them clear and close. Then push on, go forward, and accomplish them.

To take a life, *your* life, and steer it in the direction you would like, toward the career you want and the fulfillment of your dreams, is the journey—the only *real* journey. No matter how rich or successful you think you are, unless you harness your dreams and continue to grow and develop, a boring, sedentary life will set in. Similarly, those who think they are at the bottom of the barrel, who feel apathetic and numb or think their lives have no chance—they, too, can turn it around and change. Whether you feel you're successful, at the bottom of the barrel, or somewhere in between, it's time to shake yourself into action and onto the road of your dreams.

INTRODUCTION

Do you know that a career requires superhuman effort? Do you know how and from where we summon this superhuman effort?

There is a tremendous power in man, in our ability to alter, move, and redesign the world around us. We have seen man move mountains, alter the course of rivers, travel to the moon, conquer illness, build cities, construct pyramids in the desert, and create art—accomplishments that could be considered superhuman. We've also seen people who have survived after being trapped in a collapsed building, or stranded on a deserted mountaintop after a plane crash, or abandoned at sea after a shipwreck. With no apparent chance of making it through, they cling to another energy—a superhuman resolve—and survive, against all odds.

In all the above cases, I believe that spirit kept individuals going and instilled a will to live, a fierce desire to survive, a passion to create. Yet I don't think this elevated energy is any different from that required to get your career where you want it to be. The same kind of intensity, passion, and ferocity used to build the Parthenon or survive an accident is needed to propel action toward the realization of your dreams.

I believe that the true nature of man is spiritual, and that spirit is the bedrock on which intention and hard work are built. I embrace spirituality, but I'm most interested in the tangible results of this somewhat intangible empowerment. I'm most interested in that last reach for a pocket of air, in the physical effort required to locate a pine needle to suck for nourishment, in the search for a more secure grip on the wreckage. I'm most interested in spirituality that leads to *actions* that enhance people's lives.

In researching this book, I looked up "spiritual" and "action" in a Webster's 1904 dictionary I bought for a buck in a New York bookstore—the best dictionary I've ever seen. Aside from the more accepted definitions of spirituality as something ethereal, I found the following:

> **spirit,** *n.* [L. *spirare,* to breathe; the primary sense is to rush or drive.] 1. Eager desire. 2. A person of activity; a man of life, vigor, or enterprise. 3. That which hath energy; the quality which manifests life, activity, or the power of strongly affecting other bodies.

> **spiritual,** *adj.* 1. To animate with vigor. 2. Ardor; heat; stimulating quality.

action, *n.* 1. A driving; hence the state of acting or moving; exertion of power or force, as when one body acts on another. 2. An act or thing done; a deed. 3. *The actions of men are the best interpretation of their thoughts.*—Locke.

I was struck by the similarity of these definitions. Often, the attainment of "spirituality" brings to mind the image of a placid individual, motionless and meditative, sitting for hours in the lotus position under a bodhi tree. Many see the word as having a religious connotation. I don't negate these meanings, but I see spirit more in terms of persistence, tenacity, passion, involvement, caring, and resolve. Spirit is what pushes people to accomplish the impossible.

I've seen people wait years for some spiritual motivation to do things for their career. But waiting accomplishes nothing. Much better alternatives are simple actions and concrete tasks. These will move you forward and activate your spirit. That spirit, that energy will in turn promote bolder actions, and on you go.

From meditation to space travel, from cooking to painting, from farming to prayer, there is spiritual motivation accompanied by action. Is it farfetched to believe that in a custodian's work there is a spirituality that not only motivates the action of the broom's path across the floor but is nourished by it? Spirit and action coexist and are synonymous. They are interdependent in definition and experience. This book seeks to help uncover and realize dreams through the white-hot fusion of spirit and action.

DREAMS: REAL OR FANCIED?

Are you ready for this? From Webster's 1904 dictionary:

> *DREAM: To deceive, to delude. Ghost, apparition. Deceptive illusion. Living in dreams without the ability to move. Castle in the air.*

Watch out, friend, or you may achieve your dreams only in your dreams. In the real world it's easy to let dreams stay in the dreamworld. Does this fertile dream of yours—unique, exciting, startling, that was to turn the world topsy-turvy—remain only an illusion, a puff of smoke?

> *DREAM: To procrastinate. To perform indolently as in a dream. Idle speculator. Dream away the time.*

Are you asking, "Hey, what's he telling us? I thought dreams were great"? I'm telling you if you want to realize your dreams, you'd better know how tough it is. You'd better know that opinions exist in direct opposition to our dreams. Surprisingly, some of these opinions can be found within ourselves; others are there in the world at large. It's not like you can walk down the boulevard and say, "I've got a dream," and everybody will drop what they're doing and say, "Hey, baby! It's the Dreamer. How ya doin', my man? How 'bout hittin' us with some of your dream?" Maybe it will happen this way, but don't sit in the depot waiting for that train. More likely you'll hear some fancy Dan say, "Oh no, not the Dreamer again. You know, I gotta tell you, you're not all that well wrapped. Here's to you. . . ." Whereupon, with startling aplomb, His Lordship proceeds posthaste to urinate upon your shoes—and your dream.

Martin Luther King, Jr., said, "I have a dream." His dream was practical, down-to-earth, easy to understand. His coast-to-coast pronouncement of his dream and persistent efforts to push it forward made it real. His concept was specific: Ride at the front of the bus, sit at the lunch counter, drink from any water fountain, vote. His dream was not idle. His dream was not a castle in the air. His dream was not a fancy. As we know, there were those who opposed him. There were huge obstacles to his dream. The statistics indicate that his dream for African-Americans is still a long way from completion. We all still have a lot of work left to do to fulfill his dream, his practical vision necessary for the realization of America, and for people everywhere. But because his dream was specific, real, and passionate, it inspires us to go on seeking the "promised land."

Dreams are great, but do you know what you have to go through to realize a dream? As an example, have you ever tried to achieve a dream in theater or film? I have. And what happens is the same kind of roof-caving-in, monstrous, obstinate, potentially glorious, potentially catastrophic madness that occurs in most professions when you try to accomplish a dream. You'd better be bringin' some hammers, some artistic artillery, and some unshakable plans. You'd better come with some real purpose, some dedication, and some potent vitamins. Because you need all this to get you ready for some inevitable, dream-eroding trouble. It's not as if you can just walk in and say, "Mr. Producer, here I am with my dream," and Mr. Producer dashes to his checkbook to fund your fantasies. "Come, let's help this boy, he has a dream" is not necessarily the pithy maxim you will hear. Not to mention our ever-present, indispensable advisors, helpers, family, and Uncle Bob—our personal critics, who are not customarily heard to comment, "Have you heard about Charlie? He has a dream. Let's go encourage him!" Not likely.

DREAMLIKE: Insubstantial, vague, shadowy. Idle, as a dream. A vain fancy, a wild conceit. To dream away, to waste in idle thoughts. A man lost in wild imagination.

This is a practical world, the "show me" planet. You need to make things real. You need to put it out there to be seen and experienced. It takes hard work to transform your dream into a physical reality. And get ready to be knocked down, because if you're out there chasing a dream, you're bound to bite the dust. You need to learn how to get back up. I don't know anybody who pursues a dream who isn't going to bite the dust at least once. You have to get up, dust yourself off, straighten out your chops, get your ass in gear, gas up your tank, and jump back into the fray. Getting up once is tough. Getting up a hundred times is ridiculous. Well, be prepared, because that's the way it might be.

DREAMER: A sluggard. A mope. Negligent. Misty, dim, indistinct, or cloudy.

That's a big one. Doesn't it feel that way to you when you dream? Cloudy? A little murky? Dreaming can be a misty thing—imprecise and thus unattainable.

If our dreams are so wonderful, why aren't they happening? What's wrong? As I was researching this, looking up definitions and writing them down, I felt stronger with each definition because even though I hadn't looked at dreams in this seemingly negative way before, I knew it was the truth. Not that dreams aren't beautiful, as we all know they can be. Dreams are fantastic. Dreams can be the signals, the signposts to our possibilities. Dreams, as they relate to our desires, our goals, our plans, and eventually our careers, are the elusive subject that fascinates many of us. How to harness our dreams and put them in hand is the territory that I will be exploring in this book, looking to uncover some pay dirt hidden in the rocks.

Within each of us there is the potential to realize our dreams. *Potential,* however, can be a negative term if we think of it as something that justifies our waiting instead of getting what we want now. The world looks negatively upon your dream until it is put into action. Then, and only then, does it become something of substance. Not idle thought, not a gossamer thing, but a sharp, vivid, well-tuned racing car. It becomes something real, alive. That's why *Dreams Into Action* is so important.

This is the first in a series of exercises in this book. They will serve you best if you write out your answers. In each exercise, take an honest look and answer as you see it. If you have any difficulty answering, come back to that exercise after you have read more.

EXERCISE

State your dream. Just let it out. Say it aloud. Write it down.

THE FLIGHT OF A HAWK

I was once invited to talk to a high school graduating class about careers, and that's when I first looked up the definition and began to study different meanings of that word. Here are a couple of beauties from the 1904 Webster's:

> CAREER: *Originally the course on which a race is run. A road, a racing course. In falconry, the flight of a hawk, about 120 yards.*

Now, we also know a career is the occupation you choose and your life's work, but there are these other definitions, which can open up a deeper understanding of the word and hence a greater involvement in that whole sphere of life. Career is a life's work, a profession, an occupation, but also . . .

> CAREER: *To cause to rush freely and swiftly. Charge, flight, achievement, passage. A career was originally the ground for a race, especially for knights charged in tournament or battle. The way or route over which one passes.*

Here's another angle:

CAREER OF A HORSE: A short gallop or run at full or great speed. Via, a road for cars.

And finally:

When a ship is decked out in all her canvas, every sail swelled, and careering gaily over the curling waves, how gallant, how lofty she appears.

Isn't that wonderful? Now, how many of our journeys are like a decked-out ship, careering over the curling swells? And how many are like a rock plummeting to the bottom of the deep, dark sea? *Glub, Glub, Glub.* That's the rock sinking to the bottom. There's no "careering over the waves" when the journey becomes such a serious and significant matter. Life becomes tight, heavy, knotted, inflexible—a rock with no flight possible.

Let's look at one young woman who is working in advertising. She's been interested in acting ever since she took a few acting classes in college. She now wants to take the plunge and actively pursue her dream. What would Mom and Dad think? *Glub.* What would her friends think? *Glub.* How could she afford to do this and keep up all her credit card payments? *Glub, Glub.* Tight. Fearful. Complaining. Immovable. Her dream drowns and each day becomes a paralyzing nightmare. Fear, worry, and the "practical considerations" of our friends and family are anathema to a successful career and the full gallop it demands.

If you're going to "career gaily over the waves," don't sit back waiting for approval, waiting for something to take place. *Move.* You must do things for your career even when you don't know exactly what to do. Don't just sit at home and go, "Wah!" bemoaning your fate. Do something. Anything, really. Move the furniture. Play some salsa on the CD player. Anything. But better, do something specific for your career. Make a phone call. Write a letter. Devise a plan for a promotion.

My brother-in-law was a commercial housepainter for many years and decided at age fifty-one that his life was not interesting enough. He liked painting, but it didn't give him a kick in the ass. He had a fondness for the old—old auto parts, chains, tools, scraps, spikes. One day he got a torch and from these ingredients started welding together unusual sculptures. He took an art course. Now sculpture is his vocation and painting his avocation.

My friend Joe Stern was an actor until he was thirty-five. He made a decision at that time that he was through with acting. He announced this to himself aloud. He wasn't in a career crisis, but he felt strongly it was time to move on. He wanted to be a film or television producer. Moved by this decision, he wrote letters and reached contacts and after six weeks he had his first producing job. Later he became the producer for the successful television show *Law and Order* and opened his own theater company in Los Angeles. You can't wait until somebody else does it, until "they" call you. Waiting is for the birds. You have to pursue, you have to chase your dream, whether it's a childhood desire or one that hits you in the middle of life.

A career is a race, and it's yours to win. It's not something that happens to you. *You* determine its course. Not your parents. Not your college career advisor. Not your MasterCard balance. Not practicality. Not common sense. It's not what "they" approve of or what "they" tell you to do. Ultimately, it's up to you, and you'll win only by tapping into your passion, your desires, your humor, and your tenacity. It's your trip.

EXERCISE

Write down anything that makes your dream more defined, by relating it to a specific career.

CAREER CONCEPT: THE BEAT OF YOUR LIFE

You'll do better in show business, in any business, if you have an idea of how it should go: a career concept. You need something to direct you to your goals and help you pursue them in a systematic, deliberate, persevering fashion. A career concept acts as a map to your destination.

> *Concept is an idea formulated from information, need, and desire, to guide one in the visualization and execution of a work of art or anything else. Concept is a plan.*

The first step in creating a career concept is to write down what you want. Whether or not you're aware of exactly what this is, write down as much as you know. When you put things on paper, they become real. You need to get your dream out of your head, onto paper, and into your hands where you can work with it.

Along with my other activities as a director, teacher, and writer, I wanted a career as a painter. I was clear about it, and after seeing an exhibition in New York, I simply wrote down: "I went to a gallery today on Madison Avenue. I liked the painter's work. I can paint like that. I can do as well. My visual sense is pretty strong. I'd like to paint, and I'm going to do it." Then I launched myself into many hours of intensive painting. Six months later I won the Emily Lowe Competition, entered by nine thousand painters. That simple statement launched my painting career and has kept me alive as a visual artist for thirty years.

So write it down. Get yourself some chalk, a Bic, a pencil, a marker, a Waterman, or a quill. Scratch it, scrawl it, type it, etch it, carve it. Dare yourself. Be arrogant. The statement I wrote about my painting sounds somewhat arrogant, but arrogant literally means "claiming for oneself." Arrogance, using the proper definition, is a must for claiming your idea, your concept, and your own power to accomplish your goals. Simply put it down on paper.

Concept can determine the style and look of a thing.

When you first formulate your career concept and try to nail it down, you may have some difficulty. You have to be specific. It's hard to face specifics, but you must. Define everything, no matter how small it seems. Write down every detail. This detailed concept helps you to define what you are after, gives you something exact to strive for, and guides you in the precise steps to get what you want.

If you're an actor and want a TV series, what type? A tough police drama, a hospital series, or a sitcom? What kind of character do you want to play? What director do you want to work with? Be precise. If you're a restaurateur, what do you want? An Italian family-style place? Gourmet French? Or a hamburger stand? What do you want it to look like? Homey or new chic? What's your budget? How many employees can you afford? You need more money? Plan a bigger budget. Never let money dictate the boundaries of your dream. You can't follow your bliss, baby, if you've got one eye feverishly looking over your shoulder at the smoking checkbook on the desk.

Don't get into this vague idea about wanting to be a successful actor, a successful businessperson, a successful architect. That doesn't cut it. It's like saying, "I just want a car. You know, a car, any kind." No. Make it clear. What make? What year? What model? What color? Know what you want. Make it real. Buy it. Then you can drop the top, hit the interstate, and start cruising.

A career concept will give you the overall picture of your career, but it's important that the picture is not some impressionistic, veiled notion. The picture needs to be sharp. Again, know what you want. The more you know, the more you'll know what to do. If it ends up as a long dissertation, don't panic. Hone it down. State it simply. And when you get your career concept down on paper—clean, lean, mean, focused, practical, and ultimately do-able—you're on your way. The rest is just doing it.

When you write down your career concept, you

may stir up your overly emotional psychology. Facing and dealing with your career can be upsetting, especially if you're not where you want to be. This exercise is not about dealing with past disappointments, failures, or psychological blocks. All those papers should be sent to Dr. Freud in Vienna. What your paper should contain is a career concept that will punch through the loud, leering faces of doubt, fear, and victimhood.

This is the age of psychology. Don't buy into it. You don't need to lead with your problems. Leaning on your problems diffuses your career thrust. Some people actually get so creative and involved with their negativity that this downbeatness becomes the theme of their life and then the justification and excuse for their failure.

I was watching Paul Newman on the tube and he was asked a question by a young actor: "Mr. Newman, having come to your age and having accomplished what you have, is there any more, any kind of a dream to do something more?" Newman replied, "There's something still there. I don't know what, but it will surface." So a career concept is there even for the most successful, at whatever age.

A concept must have energy. It can't be a stale piece of bread that lifelessly just says, "I'm a concept." No, it must be alive and vigorous to propel movement and action. When you become bogged down, the concept will free you and drive you along the way. Your enthusiasm will flag. Obstacles will appear all around you, as if the whole world is saying no to what you want to accomplish. The going will get dusty, discouraging, and downright rough. Partner, you're going to need a kick start once in a while. When the trail is blocked, you need another way through the canyons. So it's up to you, as always. You have to come up with an on-the-spot, newfangled idea or two to push you through.

An idea is a thought created to resolve a problem, or a way to accomplish an action or intention.

You may be moving along briskly with your concept working nicely when it all comes to a screeching halt. STOP! Zero. Nada. Zilch. No question about it, you're not going to go from now until they put you in a box never failing, never getting blocked, always perfect, just walking through life with every obstacle parting before you like the Red Sea. Even with the clearest, most alive concept, you are going to have problems. There's nothing wrong with that. In fact, problems and their solutions are what keep the journey unpredictable and alive. Problems keep your blood surging. Don't be thrown by them. Don't give up. Be on your toes. Be nimble. Be quick. When you hit a problem, a stop, you've got to come up with an idea to get out of the jam. Concept and ideas need to interact. A concept will tell you where to go, and your ideas will keep you on course.

When you get knocked down, and on planet Earth at one time or another you most certainly will, you need to act like a boxer. Get up off the canvas, get back on your feet, wipe the rosin off your gloves, and ask the referee, "Where is he? Let me at him!" Then you're back at it again. And no "no's." If you want to accomplish something positive, there can't be a "no" in your vocabulary. You are not to be stopped. This actually defines a pro—someone who accomplishes what he or she has decided to do.

Let's say you've decided to take a trip. Concept: a leisurely motoring tour of the mountains to view the late fall foliage. But in the middle of your trip a blizzard hits. You're stuck in snow up to your navel. Idea: Put chains on the tires. That works for a while, but the storm worsens. Idea: There is a warm, cozy lodge just up the road. Hit it. Next day, sunny enough to melt the snow. Off you go. Is this all too simple for you? Well, it works. Ideas put concept once again in full flourish.

I heard a damn good career concept when Robert DeNiro spoke to one of my acting classes and said, "I got into acting as a way toward self-expression." Simple. You can see him trying to be more and more expressive in every part. He'll go to any length—gain seventy pounds, shave his head, anything—to overcome any inhibitions, to be more expressive. He lives through that expressiveness in a very personal way. That's his concept. In the same way, your career concept cries out to be personal. It's yours. You have to feel it, have a passion for it, connect with it so that you work and live to get it done.

Your concept must be so clear and so strong within

you, your desire so fiery, that no obstacle is too great. Write it out. Make it yours. Believe in it. Be passionate. It is your Declaration of Independence. Emblazon your career concept on your heart and let it be the beat of your life.

EXERCISE

Write out your career concept. Be bold, but be specific. Don't deal in psychology. Hone it down to a workable, practical, do-able concept.

THE LAUNCHING PAD

Here's a simple thing you can do that you will find helpful in getting your career off the ground. Get yourself a sturdy, well-ordered desk where you can work to organize your career concept and plan your daily activities without any distractions or interruptions. This desk will function as your launching pad. It should be well placed in the room—a bright spot, uncluttered, maybe even with a nice view. Often just creating this kind of space can give you a sense of confidence and power. And remember, it's your space. Don't share it with others. If you're living with someone, get your own phone, your own answering machine, your own desk.

I once had an experience with a very fine actress who felt her career was not progressing. She was talented, beautiful, and had done some good work, but something was wrong. Her life at home was filled with distractions from family and friends. I told her to get a desk and create her own space. She placed it in a private part of the house. She set the ground rules with her family and friends. When she was at work at her desk she was not to be disturbed.

From her new operating base, she was able to get organized. She began making telephone calls, setting up appointments, scheduling meetings. She had once been in a Scorsese film, and he was getting ready to cast his latest. She called, but he told her there was no role for her. I suggested she write to him and say she would play any role. She was not concerned about the size of the part, or the money. This was all part of her new operating procedure from her new power base. She got herself organized and focused. It worked. She got a part.

EXERCISE

Complete this Launching Pad checklist:
___ Desk
___ Telephone
___ Calendar
___ List of contacts
___ Stationery
___ Dictionary

CHOICES

Every moment of life demands a choice. Your career concept requires you to make a choice, and day to day, the minutiae of life demand that you make a choice either to move your career along or to slow it down to a stop. Do I write that letter I've been putting off, or do I turn on the tube? Choice. Am I too pissed off to call my guy and make up? Am I too tired to go to this meeting? Choice. Too lazy to go over that research material? Too frightened to finish my income taxes? Just choice. The important choices of your life are often the minor ones. They're not only the ones that you live with day to day, but also the ones that provide the training and discipline for making the big decisions.

When you have completed the job interview, the business meeting, or the actor's audition, and you're not satisfied with what you did, do you stop on your way out the door, turn around, and go back and say, "I've got a problem with what just went down. Can we discuss it?" Or, "Can we look at that contract once more?" Or, "Can I hit that again? I didn't like my audition." Or do you bow your head, get in your car, and go home to bury your face in a paisley blanket and weep? All choices.

If you feel trapped in a situation—unable to make a decision, unable to make a choice—and feel you can't do anything about it, go to the beach. Get out of it for a while. Take a walk in the woods. Get away from it. Look at the options. Put the options down on paper, get them out of your head.

I had a friend, a computer engineer, who was trying to decide between staying in his job—stable, good money, stock options, growing company—or taking an offer from a new firm that involved the same money but a lot of travel to Russia and creativity regarding deals for imports and such. What I suggested to him was to write down on paper the positive and negative aspects of the Russia gig, and the positive and negative aspects of his current gig. The reason I made sure he addressed the current gig is that people can too easily say, "I know my situation, I know what I've got," and thereby miss some important points. Write it out.

If and when you have a decision to make, a choice, take out a yellow pad, a pen, and one piece of paper for each option. Draw a line down the middle of each page and write at the top the name of each option. Write the positive aspects on one side, the negative aspects on the other. Write everything you can possibly think of in either category. Everything. Do that for each option you have. Evaluate the negative versus the positive. Study your answers. Which option helps your family the most? Which one presents you with the most benefits in the future, both spiritually and materially, both short-term and long-term? Then decide.

Many people make decisions based on how they feel. Don't base your choice on feeling, but on the good and bad points you write down on paper. This simple method is a much more effective way to help yourself make a choice. Choice is the most important part of the whole deal. So make it, and have fun making it. Like life itself, making a choice is a game, so have fun arriving at your decisions. Then "career gaily over the waves."

EXERCISE

1) Review three choices you've made recently, and reevaluate them in accord with what's been discussed in this chapter.

2) Select three impending decisions and make your choice using the techniques discussed above.

THE PERFECTION SYNDROME

If you think you've got to make the absolutely right choice, you can get trapped and end up making no choice at all. That's getting stuck in what I call the perfection syndrome. You contend that you can't fully commit yourself to make this or that choice because you don't believe it is a perfect decision. Only one problem: There is no perfect choice. But you don't want to do anything unless it is the perfect . . . And round and round it goes. How does it end? No choice.

Laminated within the clean, elegant, solid lines of the perfect choice lies built-in failure. It goes like this: You want to repaint your living room. Should you choose eggshell white or pearl gray? You're so picky about your choice, it needs to be so perfect, that after many rejections and fluctuations you arrive at the threshold of your choice, exhausted, depleted, and shaky. Finally you haltingly, shakily execute your hair-splitting choice in some intense, desperate fashion. You say, "All right, to hell with it, pearl gray."

As you are about to begin painting, you look at the room fearfully, knowing the color you've chosen just doesn't measure up. Instantly you trample your choice with all the criticism you possess. Eggshell white? Pearl gray? Lunar blue? You desperately start looking at the paint samples again. Why? You've made a choice that's just not perfect. The eggshell would have gone so much better with the beige carpet. "Oh God, it's not right. Not right!" So what? What's the big deal? It's just one choice, you're capable of many. Don't be paralyzed by the picayune perfectionist lying within you, who wants it just right or not at all. Paint it. If you're unhappy, repaint it. Make your choice and go with it.

All our lives we've listened to the uptight voices of caution—parents, teachers, ministers, friends—tell us, "Be careful, watch it, look out now. You're going overboard." They are pretending to be helpful. "We want you to do your best. We want to help you to be right, to be perfect." This is not all of their intent. Hiding their actual motive under the banner of helpfulness, these voices of caution would rather stop you than have you embarrass them. What they're actually saying is, "Please don't make us look bad. What you're doing is not to our taste. It's not acceptable behavior." Propriety, sensibility, modesty, decorum, convention, don't-rock-the-boat—all are watchwords, often unspoken, lying beneath the laminated veneer of demanded perfectionism.

I believe the perfection syndrome is a major problem in today's society, and it plays a role in any area of life where you're experiencing difficulty. How many people have within them an idea of the perfect job, the perfect mate, the perfect parents, the perfect acting class, the perfect self, yet consider themselves to be light-years from that utopia? They become so overwhelmed by the dark chasm between reality and their ideal that instead of working to narrow the gap, they do nothing. They go into apathy. Another friend of mine owns a really terrible car, a beat-up Toyota that is always unwashed and in disrepair. I know that his dream car is a BMW convertible, and that the difference between his junker and the BMW is so considerable that he makes no effort to improve the junker. But I believe that the greater the effort he puts into improving his Toyota, the closer he will come to getting the BMW. That's the justice of this world.

EXERCISE

List five areas of your life where you're in a perfection syndrome, and describe how you can take steps to pull yourself out of this tendency and improve those areas with real and practical actions.

As a postscript to this section, I asked my editor to try this exercise. He gave me four areas where he has a problem with the perfection syndrome: (1) women, with whom he feels he needs to be Cary Grant to get a date; (2) acting, where his desire to act "correctly" inhibits his ideas; (3) a staff position he holds, where he's afraid to make a mistake; and (4) piano playing— he's a terrific pianist but sometimes gets obsessed with playing "perfectly." He was stumped for a fifth area. I asked, "What about your parents?"

"Oh, no, I used to have a perfection thing with them, being the perfect kid and all that, but I gave that up a while ago."

"You talk to them?"

"No."

"So you backed off?"

"Well . . ."

"You don't know what to do with them. They're so far from your ideal of parents that you just avoid them. Avoidance is not a choice. Avoiding makes you ineffectual just when you're trying to resolve something. The reason you don't want to admit this is because you would have to confront them."

"You mean in person?" We both cracked up laughing.

Breaking Down Old Systems

At some point you've got to cut yourself free from what you think are your opinions but are really the opinions of others. These views are held in place to please others, to make you more acceptable, more likable, and to avoid arguments and trouble. In avoiding trouble you are actually running over yourself, your thoughts, your beliefs, and in the bargain insulating yourself from life's real experiences.

Let's say you see a movie and you disagree with your boyfriend's opinion about it, but you let it slide. As he speaks about it, you swallow your own opinion and adopt his view. A few days later you give his views for yours when a friend asks you what you thought about the movie. If you follow this path, you may find yourself ten years later in an unfulfilled relationship. This screwed-up relationship is your payback for ten years of not saying what you feel about a movie, and about God knows what else. At some point, at some time, about something, you have to start saying what you feel in a relationship.

Your borrowed opinions may have little if anything to do with who you really are and who you want to be. You are adopting these views automatically, or they are adopting you. You sanction their use as if they were your own thoughts and feelings. Look at yourself closely. In how many of your views on race, religion, art, sex, business, etc. do you find echoes of your parents' views? Your friends'? Your spouse's? How many have you sifted through to determine whether you really agree with them or not? Are you living a script written by somebody else? You have to write your own script. You have to discover your own values, your own viewpoints, your own passions. You have to cut that umbilical cord to your parents and others, and separate your own unique point of view from those of your nice, conforming, safe, status quo friends and family. When you put your stamp on what you think and feel, you are heading toward your own uniqueness. You don't have to give up loving those who have influenced you, but it's now time to go on and find your own way. As you move on you may actually find love gained.

The unwillingness to give up old ways of thinking, old ways of doing things, old ways of seeing yourself grounds you in place like an anchor. You don't "career over the waves." You sink. These opinions that are not yours weaken who you are. Meanwhile, inside of us there are screams about not achieving our dreams. To accomplish anything in this world you need to believe in your way. You need to have confidence in what you think and feel and, with your power, get done what you want done. I'm not suggesting a revolution, but an evolution. To become more productive and effective, you may have to change and evolve, move, give up old ways of thinking so a new, stronger you can emerge.

EXERCISE

Get a pad and pencil and write down a few opinions you have about movies, politics, world affairs, relationships, and food, and maybe even opinions about yourself. Look the list over. Roll it around a bit. Check it out. Are these views yours or someone else's? It's up to you to decide. Keep them or shed them?

HAMAL

HAMAL (pronounced hah-MAHL): *Turkish word meaning the lowest common day-worker. Especially those who haul heavy loads on their backs. A beast of burden.*

An actor onstage in acting class, pushing a broom, reveals that when he was a young boy his father taught him to push a broom. He's been working as some kind of janitor ever since. Even now, while training as an actor, he helps clean up the theater, continuing to pursue the technique of the broom. This discussion follows:

MILTON: How did you feel about giving up your music? And going back to pushing the broom at your father's glass shop?

STUDENT: I felt like a failure to myself.

MILTON: Tell anybody about it?

STUDENT: No. In fact, I haven't said any of this to anybody.

MILTON: Anybody discourage you from pursuing your music thing?

STUDENT: Well, my family considered it a hobby. When I quit the glass business, I was living on twenty dollars a week and just played the guitar and learned all day. They were very happy when I quit playing music.

MILTON: Anybody in your family encourage you? I mean, when you went home to visit, when they laid the mashed potatoes and gravy on your plate, were they looking at you like some twenty-dollar-a-week, off-the-wall musician? Or did they greet you with wreaths of victory?

STUDENT: No. It was always more like, "What are you doing with your life? When are you going to get your shit together and come back to the glass shop?"

MILTON: So they were actively involved in getting you away from this music thing and back to the glass thing.

STUDENT: Yeah. They discouraged me every time.

MILTON: Who was the major discourager?

STUDENT: I believe it was my father. I mentioned

to my mother that whenever I was in the glass business, doing whatever my father wanted me to do, they were all behind me. But whenever I strayed from that, they were completely against me.

MILTON: I understand. Did you ever tell him how he discouraged you from music?

STUDENT: No.

MILTON: Tell him now.

STUDENT: I should write him a letter.

MILTON: You could tell him a few things now if you like. We can improvise, put somebody up there for you to talk to. They can be your father, or you can just talk to the wall if you like.

STUDENT: Oh God, I hadn't thought about that.

MILTON: Go ahead, tell him right now. From there. Just tell him.

STUDENT: *(Softly.)* I don't really know what to say.

MILTON: Try.

STUDENT: *(To his father.)* You know, I think I
             know why you didn't want me to go
             into the music business. It was because
             of Ron Smith being a guitar player and
             playing all over honky-tonks, and get-
             ting drunk and raising hell all the time,
             and not showin' up for work. That's
             the only thing you had to compare a
             musician with—some drunk who
             played honky-tonks. You had no idea
             about how music made me feel. About
             how maybe I could have a life besides
             hard work from sunup to sundown.
             Music was something that moved me.
             I can't even explain in words how
             music made me feel.

MILTON: Tell him how it made you feel to give up
             music.

STUDENT: *(To his father.)* I've always wanted to
             do the things you wanted me to. I've
             always wanted to be perfect in your
             eyes. But I can't live my life through
             you. I never wanted to do anything
             more in my life than play music.
             Without your support I never felt good

about myself. I felt like a complete failure in your eyes. When I quit playing, I hated you for it. I still hate you for it. I don't understand.... *(In tears.)* Even though you say you're behind me now, you're not. I know you're not. I can't even talk to you on the phone without you wanting me to come back. I want to talk to you. *(Through the tears.)* I don't feel like pushing the fucking broom anymore. I do work hard. I work hard. I worked hard at my music. Whether you know it or not, you destroyed all my confidence.

MILTON: Tell him about how some part of him died in you when you put the music down.

STUDENT: *(To his father.)* I've never met anybody who knew you who had anything bad to say about you. It made me feel like you were the best father in the whole world. When you drove me away from what I felt passionate about, I wished I had another father. I wished you were not my father. I wish I could find respect for you again. But I don't respect you.

MILTON: What could he do to regain that respect? Is there anything he could do? I mean, would a big ol' classic 1957 gull-wing convertible Cadillac do it?

STUDENT: *(Laughing.)* That's his car, not mine.

MILTON: So tell him what he could do. . . . Is there anything you could tell him to do? And then maybe you'd consider, just consider, the possible reaffirmation of some degree of respect.

STUDENT: *(To his father.)* The only thing . . . the only thing I know is if you could just take me in your arms and give me a real hug, and say to me for the first time that you love me for who I am. . . . I don't care if you approve of what I do. I can't tell you in words what I feel when I come home to see you once a year. You want to shake my hand. I don't want a fucking handshake.

MILTON: So if he did this, you'd consider, just consider, the possibility of some reaffirmed respect? Is that true?

STUDENT: If he did it from his heart.

MILTON: Good. Just stay right where you are. Do you know that speech "To be or not to be . . ."?

STUDENT: I'll probably forget it . . .

MILTON: Go ahead with what you're feeling. Right now. Don't worry . . . just a little piece of it . . .

STUDENT: To be . . . or not to be. That is the question. Whether 'tis nobler . . .

MILTON: In the mind . . .

STUDENT: Nobler in the mind . . .

MILTON: To suffer . . .

STUDENT: Whether 'tis nobler in the mind to suffer the slings and arrows of outrageous fortune, or take arms against a sea of troubles, and by opposing, end them.

MILTON: To die, to sleep . . .

STUDENT: To die, to sleep no more. And by a

sleep to say we end the heartache and the thousand natural shocks that flesh is heir to . . .

MILTON: Yeah. 'Tis a consummation devoutly to be wished.

STUDENT: 'Tis a consummation devoutly to be wished. To die, to sleep. To sleep, perchance to dream . . .

MILTON: Tell him. Tell him. Say it to your father.

STUDENT: For in that sleep of death what dreams may come? There's a respect that makes calamity of so long life.

MILTON: Tell him about the humiliation . . .

STUDENT: For those would bear the whips and scorns of time . . . *(He snaps the broomstick over his knee.)*

MILTON: Okay. How're you doing?

STUDENT: This is fun.

(Laughter from the class.)

MILTON: *(To the class.)* Yeah. Now, does every-body here understand what we're doing? He took his personal feelings and put them directly into a play, *Hamlet.* It's an acting tool.

Now, the basis for this particular personal monologue is the hamal attitude that enters into people and they feel like beasts of burden, even if some of them are living in palaces. Their surroundings don't necessarily make for healthy internal life, self-esteem, or confidence. You have to deal with the hamal. I don't know any great artist, any real human being who is a hamal. I know a lot of great artists and wonderful people who have made their way from the hamal to something greater. Some guys still feel like hamals even though they have big offices and make four hundred thousand a year. Payroll doesn't prevent the hamal, and the broom doesn't make a hamal. There's no big deal about pushing a broom. What makes a hamal is what lives inside you.

There is a custodian who works in SoHo who told my brother one day,

"People wonder how I can pick up trash and garbage, just clean up. I tell them I feel like I'm really contributing. But I can't tell one of my helpers this. He just doesn't understand. You see, I take pride." This man walks around the neighborhood with a singing strut that makes him look as if he owns all of SoHo. Feeling like a hamal, or having one dwell in some corner of your character, is an attitude that can be changed.

(To the actor.) I love what you did with the broom. The broom is your father. The broom is giving up your music, giving up your dreams. The broom is the hamal, and you broke it. We could have this broom in *Hamlet.* The push-broom *Hamlet.*

STUDENT: Well, I know how to do that. I push it every morning. Right outside there in the alleyway.

MILTON: There is no big deal about pushing a broom; it's how you feel when you push it.

STUDENT: That's true. Sometimes I like pushing it.

MILTON: I mean, if you never push a broom again, that's great. It's also great if you push a broom whenever you want, and take pride in it. That's when you become Hamlet, the prince.

EXERCISE

Make a list of where you have been a hamal—in your job, relationships, or family—and what you did to get out of it. Be as specific as possible. Now list where you're currently a hamal and what you can do to get out of it. Be tough on yourself, but don't bury yourself under the baggage you find.

Put Your Ear Up and Let the Guy Talk Into It

How many of you have a problem with reading? Whether it's reading books, a prospectus, newspapers, magazines, scripts, contracts, or the minutes of a meeting, my guess is half of you are having some difficulty. This chapter may seem like a digression, but reading proficiency is the entrance point to any skill. It is central to the heart and soul of any career, any life.

Now, I don't want to take all your television remotes away from you, but with very few exceptions, our society does not read enough. Reading is going out of style because of television and our fast-paced lifestyles. The television remote allows us to rush feverishly from channel to channel, looking for anything that will absorb our interest for twenty seconds. Reading is a skill. With reading you've got to knuckle down, you've got to be patient.

Here's my definition of reading: "Put your ear up and let the guy talk into it."

That's it. That's what it is to me. It's that simple. Nothing more. Society teaches us that if we can't read, we're dumb, slow, or stupid. When these judgments of intellect are attached to reading, reading gets a distorted significance. Reading is communication. That's all it is. Someone talks. You put your ear up and let the guy talk into it. Don't just sit there with your judgments trying to dismiss the author. He'll tell you what the bottom line is. Just let him talk.

A couple of things can help you improve your reading skills. You've heard of golfing tips? Well, here are some reading tips. Get yourself a good dictionary. Check out different types and choose the one you like best. When you're reading, use your dictionary frequently and patiently. Get a full grasp of what you're reading, and as you go along, use the dictionary whenever necessary.

Something else to consider: If you're having a problem with reading, there could be a trauma somewhere in your past associated with it. Some teacher, some family member, some friend, someone told you, "You ain't got it, baby. You ain't got this reading thing covered. You're not smart." And this experience shook you. Maybe it shook you in front of other people. Maybe in front of your classmates at school. Maybe you went home, told someone about this trauma, and got shook up again by their reaction. "Well, son, your teacher is right. You're thirteen years old and you read like a first-grader." If you remember a traumatic incident like this, just be aware of it, and note on paper what happened and who was involved. If some specific conclusion occurred to you, then or now, put it down on paper so that it's no longer held prisoner in your head. Sample conclusion: "I felt dumb in front of my classmates, then humiliated at home. I'll never be able to read. To hell with all of them." Keep this look at the trauma simple. Don't dwell on it, and keep your notes about it clear, brief, and to the point.

A word here on dyslexia. *Lexi* means "pertaining to words" in Greek, and *dys* means "to break apart." The words break apart or rearrange themselves. So dyslexia means a disturbance of the ability to read. That's the etymology of the word. I can live with that. Unfortunately, a lot of heavy significance has been laid on the literal definition. My personal preference would be more akin to the phrase my Greek mother taught me: "I tell you something, and you stubbornly insist I told you something else." I checked this definition with two professors at the University of California at Los Angeles Language Department. They said it was perfectly acceptable. It came from common usage and from the heart. If you look at dyslexia in this way, it is possible to see that to some extent you are doing it, and you can help resolve it.

Therefore, I see dyslexia as a decision. A decision made by people themselves. It may be a decision that people are unaware they've made, but one that is perhaps closer to the surface than previously thought. I don't mean in any way to disparage the honest efforts and hard work of those who work in the important field of reading disabilities. But I believe there are times when the problem can be handled more easily and swiftly than is commonly accepted. In some cases, I believe it is possible to put an X through dyslexia.

There are, of course, serious and difficult reading disabilities that demand great finesse and patience. But with all due respect, I would like to introduce the idea that, as in the Greek expression, dyslexia is "I tell you something, and you stubbornly insist I told you something else." And with that, my simple approach to reading is: "Put your ear up and let the guy talk into it."

(CLASS DISCUSSION)

MILTON: Okay. What is reading?

STUDENT #1: Reading is closing your ear and listening to what the author has to say. . . .

MILTON: So reading is closing your ear?

STUDENT #1: Yes.

MILTON: Would you say the ear is like a door?

STUDENT #1: Yes.

MILTON: Do you close the door and listen?

STUDENT #1: You can.

MILTON: You can. What's a better way?

STUDENT #1: You open the door.

MILTON: Great. So tell me again . . .

STUDENT #1: Close your ear and listen to what the author says.

MILTON: So what do you do with this door?

STUDENT #1: Leave it open.

MILTON: Good. And this ear?

STUDENT #1: Leave it open?

MILTON: You got it. So what is reading?

STUDENT #1: Reading is putting your ear out to listen to what the author has to say.

MILTON: Almost. But remember, the door only opens when the key fits exactly. Put your ear up and let the guy talk into it. But you used the word *listen*. Words like *listen* can seem a little significant. Sounds like a command. You can say, "Listen? You want me to listen? To hell with you, I'm not gonna." And you used the word *author*. *Author* can be this big authority figure, and that can turn you off. So. No more author. Just let the guy talk into your ear, that's all.

STUDENT #1: Okay, okay. I think I got it. Reading is putting your ear up and letting the guy talk into it.

MILTON: That's it. The door's open.

(Class cheers.)

MILTON: Reading is not a test of intelligence, it's not a competitive race. If you only go one page a day while your best friend reads a novel a week, that's all right. Be patient. It will eventually go faster. Just get that one page clear and understood. Your confidence will go way up.

STUDENT #2: I'm having trouble with someone who doesn't read at all. I try to help, but he gets so angry.

MILTON: Boyfriend?

STUDENT #2: Yes.

MILTON: Just a wild guess. He's fighting it. You

can try to help in a nice way, a gentle way, a patient way, even a firm way, but in the end he will have to make the choice to improve. Or not.

STUDENT #3: When I look up words in the dictionary, I have trouble retaining their meaning.

MILTON: I'm a whiz with the dictionary. One of the ways I became a whiz was to keep looking up words until I nailed them. If you look up a word and in the definition there's another word you need to look up, don't worry, it's okay. Follow it. Take the trip. This persistence is a big part of becoming a whiz.

(END OF CLASS DISCUSSION)

This approach to reading is done in my classes, and there has been enormous improvement for the students across the board. Some have increased their interest in reading and the number of books they read by 50 percent. Others even more. So give this approach a go.

From one of my students, Lenny Citrano:

I got all the way through college without reading a book. I viewed it as a waste of time. Then one night Milton talked to our acting class about a specific approach to reading and its influence on the hamal, a person's attitude toward himself as a lowly, power-less beast of burden. That's when it dawned on me that I was feeling like the hamal. I thought every-body in the world must be smarter than me because they could read anything they wanted.

So I took Milton's tips on reading, including the pur-chase of a first-class dictionary. Milton's first sug-gestion was From Here to Eternity, *taking my time with it and looking up any words I didn't under-stand. It was pretty slow going at first, but I stuck with it, and got a real feeling of accomplishment when I finished the last page. I also realized I actu-ally enjoyed hearing what the writer, James Jones, had to say.*

The next book Milton assigned was Hemingway's For Whom the Bell Tolls. *I got stuck in the middle of that one, and dropped the ball completely. Then one day Milton asked me, "How's it going with Hemingway?" I had to tell him I'd stopped reading it. He said, "Oh no. No, you don't. Go back and fin-ish it, or we'll start to smell the hamal again." So I finished it.*

Over the past two years, I've read eighteen books. From short, fairly light two-hundred-page novels all the way to Tolstoy's gigantic Anna Karenina. *That's in addition to the twenty-four plays I've read for the play-reading class I attend. Reading is very important for me. In reading, I get a real clear picture of different places. I haven't traveled a great deal, but in a funny way now I feel I have.*

These days I always have at least one book going. I can read anything I want now. Reading has helped me tremendously, both as an actor and as a person. The hamal in me is dead, dead, dead.

EXERCISE

Buy a good dictionary. Using whatever you're reading, as you come across words you don't understand, look them up. If there are words in the definition you don't understand, follow through and look those up. Use this technique from now on, whenever you read. Even if you have an impressive college education, look up words you aren't certain about. You'll learn more than you think you could.

Free Flowing

In order to make choices, you have to be present and accounted for. You can't just show up. You have to be awake and aware of what's in front of you. Don't leave your self-esteem behind in the parking lot. Fear and attaching distorted significance to events makes you tight and rigid. You're unable to see what's actually there and so cannot respond effectively. "I *have* to get the job." "I *have* to do well at the conference." "I lose *everything* if I lose this sale." "I *have* to get this raise; I'll *die* if I don't." This is not the way. You need to be flexible. Don't press. Bring yourself to the experience. Get involved with the people you're interacting with. Listen to them. Connect with them. Talk with them. Get their point of view.

When the pressures of an interview overwhelm you to the point that you freeze up, try this: When you feel yourself going away, as difficult as it may be, check the room you're in. Feel the carpet under your feet. Notice the furniture. See the painting on the wall. Feel the pen in your hand. Observe who you are with, the tint of their hair, a blemish, or an interesting curve to their mouth. Touch something on the desk you've never touched before. See something you've never seen before. Notice the flaw in the glass you are holding. Feel the draft from the air conditioning. This technique will focus you in a meeting, dissipate your mechanical responses, and help you be awake, flexible, and effective.

Have you ever found yourself heading back to your car after a business meeting, a dental appointment, date, or even lunch with a friend having agreed to something that you now feel is impossible to live with? In poolroom vernacular, this is derisively called "eating it." You weren't able even to hear the decision much less disagree with it because you were floating in space, filled with anxiety, unable to respond. You were nervous, fearful of rocking the boat, and so you just sort of gave up and went along.

Go back to the person. Get your point of view across. Calmly discuss that dental bill you don't understand or agree with. Go back to the butcher and ask him to please take off a bit more fat. Tell your date nicely that you agree, it wasn't such a great time for you, either. Tell the head of your department, using all your know-how, that you disagree with the expansion plans, and intelligently show her why.

As an example, I'm driving to my favorite restaurant one night, no reservation. I call a couple of minutes before I get there to tell them, and on the other end of the phone I hear a little hesitation from the maître d', whom I've known for years. I offer to come back another time and he takes me up on that a little too eagerly. I'm annoyed. I wanted him to decline my offer. Then I decided, "No, I'm not going to lose this favorite dining place." Three days later I go in for lunch. I ask the maître d', "Are you okay with me? Any problems?" He replies, "Okay with you? *Oui!* Problems? Nooooo! *Mon dieu!* No problems, no problems!" I ask again. "No, no, no! *Mon cher ami!*" There are practically tears in his eyes. I'm thinking he doth protest too much, but at least I've addressed it. I haven't let it just stick, upsetting me and possibly making me drop a good restaurant. Two weeks later—short notice, no reservation—I call in. "Milton! *Mon cher!* Of course, of course, anytime . . ." Now, if I had let the first incident just sit without addressing it, if I'd eaten it, I don't think I'd be hearing the dulcet tones of "Of course, of course, anytime . . ." By the way, as an added bonus, I'm partners with him in a new restaurant.

When you make the effort to stand up and be counted in one situation, it's easier to stand up in another, then another. Each time you become more confident, and the weeds of worry don't grow around you. But if you don't stand up and you let life's situations push you around, it's easier for life to push you around the next time. Then, after a while, you're just bouncing around like a steel marble in a pinball machine, being hit randomly by situations and people. Communicating, getting your point of view across lets the world know you are there and are to be reckoned with. You become more viable as a person, more confident. It takes some doing, but if you can be there and take decisive, affirmative action, then you've got it. It's a snap. You're on your way. End of book. See ya later.

EXERCISE

1) List five situations where you "ate it," and what you could have done instead.

2) Note down any current situations where you feel you're eating it, and apply the techniques discussed in this chapter.

GETTING ALONG

Elia Kazan, the famous stage and film director, said to me when I started my directing career that 80 percent of this business is the ability to get along with people. Not talent, not brilliance, not who you know, but the ability to get along with people. Theater, film, and television are communal arts where you work in conjunction with other artists. People interacting and getting along is the engine that empowers all professions.

Getting along with people doesn't mean that you need to act as if you're running for political office and everybody must like you. You just need to be honest, direct, willing to confront (with some humor, please), and fight the battle when necessary. If you're withholding your opinions and your needs in an effort to get along with people, it will never really work. If you're not there, who the hell is? Some kind of phony card, some apology for you. That won't make it. Be yourself and give of yourself fully. That's what people will like about you. If a bit of a rebel comes out, so be it. Take risks. Don't keep your creative impulses anchored in the harbor out of fear of not getting along. Don't conform to confirm your likability.

Say what you need to say in a manner that shows your intent to solve problems, not make them. Your objective is not to fight, but rather to make a positive contribution toward some resolution. It's not to prove someone wrong, or to make you look good. Put this positive intention into your communication. First practice getting across what you mean and what you want, without rancor, in mundane, less life-threatening situations.

FIGHT: To attempt to defeat, subdue, destroy an enemy either by blows or weapons.

Who do we fight? Who's the enemy? Our partners? No. But we're about to fight with them. About what? We're fighting each other rather than the problem. Okay. What's our common problem? Fighting, fighting among ourselves, each trying to be right. Every time there's a problem, we fight. Instead of fighting each other, let's fight the real problem. So get off of me, and I'll get off of you. And let's both get on the real problem. Okay? Let's shake on it.

Regardless of the source of the conflict, keep in mind that as in all things, balance is vital. Balance between holding to your beliefs and being open enough to really get the other's point of view. If you're coming on too strong, lighten up. Remember humor. You may need to be considerate. Look at your partner. What's his or her mood? Is he or she feeling poorly today? Would it be better to deal with this problem tomorrow?

Once, when I needed more days of shooting on a film schedule, I approached my producer and perceived something different about him. I surprised him with the odd question, "What's going on with you? You seem uptight about something. Are you okay?" He seemed startled and after a moment said, "Yes, my sons are feuding. They just don't get along." My extra days of shooting seemed to fade in importance. For the first time, we had a real discussion that I think helped both of us and our relationship. He said, "I know you want more days to shoot. I can't. There just isn't the money." That was clear, and although I didn't get more time, I established a better relationship with him and a more definite picture of the shooting schedule so I would have no false hope. The fact that we went on to work on two more movies together was no doubt influenced by our having had that talk.

Cooperation is the watchword. For some, cooperation has come to mean compromise. No. *Cooperate* means "to act, or operate jointly with others toward a common purpose." Mutual effort is what it means. You are not giving up your individuality by cooperating.

For some people, fighting may be a signal of another problem. It might indicate that they are pulling back from interacting for some reason. Perhaps they're stuck and instead of cooperating, they lock up into themselves. The only thing they can give is the fight. Instead, giving in a collaborative way is what you want. Give and take. Battle together against a common foe. Together, you will solve common problems and advance individual careers. Cooperation, freely expressed, is love.

EXERCISE

1) Find two people whose cooperation you need to get a result. Use the techniques discussed above to help achieve that result.

2) Find two people with whom you're having a conflict. Find the real underlying problem that is causing you to fight each other and deal with that.

3) Find two situations, business and personal, where more cooperation is needed. Do more.

FLINCH

One of the most beautiful women in the world called one day to inquire about studying with me. I was editing a film at the time, so we met at a nearby restaurant, one of those middle-class semi-hunting-lodge-lookalike fish-and-steak joints where most of the studio people in Burbank dine. It was fall, and she was dressed in a Ralph Lauren tweed—breathtaking and more beautiful than she photographed. The meeting was warm, pleasant, flirtatious, almost sexy. I tried like hell to keep my thoughts straight and be a professional director and teacher, which in this case was not an easy task. She was desperate to improve her career, and to be thought of as a real actress. I said, and I was being truthful, that I had seen talent in her work, and definitely some improvement could easily be made. To have her talent go all the way was another matter, subject to greater uncertainty. We decided to work together in class. She was to begin in a week and would call the theater to iron out the details.

We hugged in the parking lot. She kissed me on the cheek and said she was determined to solve her problems and finally become an actress. She flashed her wonderfully seductive eyes, which felt to me at the time like a very nice punctuation. Unfortunately, it was a prelude to what was to follow.

Four days later, three days before she was to begin the class, I got a call from her, her voice even more seductive over the phone than I had remembered. She asked if I could come by her hotel. She had a problem that she didn't wish to discuss over the phone. Her voice and its promise were not something I could ignore. Like a good actor heading for a meeting about a role, I imagined all the exciting possible scenarios that would be a part of this fascinating liaison. I was at her hotel promptly at three and called her on the lobby phone, whereupon she gave me her room number, her tone more promising than ever.

Her room was the smallest I'd ever been in, and I haven't been in any smaller since. It felt as though we were in a sleeping berth on a train. And are you ready for this? (I wasn't.) She was wearing a white bikini! The first part of my fantasy was complete. But she was upset, her eyes almost tearful. She was silent for awhile, so I asked what the problem was. For the next two hours, she proceeded to tell me, in essence, the story of her life. She also indicated she had to leave town, and if I didn't mind, she would be packing during our talk. She carefully took a box from the top shelf, standing delicately and precariously in her bikini. "I have to go to Africa," she said. "It's important . . . the animals and all."

"Do you have to go now?" I asked.

"Yes, there's a real endangered species problem there."

"When do you leave?"

"In three hours."

"And how long will you remain there?"

"That's unknown," she replied.

"Will it be more than three months?"

"Possibly." She got on her knees and pulled a trunk from under a table. She looked up at me and said, "I really want to do this thing with my acting. And I will."

This mixture of stories of life, stories of Africa, stories of intent continued for two hours. Stories, stories, all bikini-clad stories. Finally I said, "I have to go."

"I was hoping you'd take me to the airport," she said.

"I'd love to. But I just can't," I said.

She took my hand in hers. "I will do the acting one day."

"Now is the day," I said. "I believe you'll either do it now, or you won't do it. Africa has been there forever. It won't disappear. Neither will your acting problems. You're hot to solve them? Solve them now."

"I can't," she said. "I have to go."

"You're running. You're avoiding. Don't."

She leaned in very close to me and whispered, "I have to."

Extremely tempted by this proximity, I quickly said, "I have to go. And I don't think you'll ever study with me." I leaned in and returned the parking lot kiss on her cheek, and was gone. Having escaped the seductive, intimate proximity of the Tom Thumb suite, I walked down the corridor of the hotel, cursing my stubborn professionalism. I realized her seductiveness was a cover, a way out, a ruse to get me to forget my responsibilities. I felt she had ducked her own responsibilities like this before. I did not want to be added to the list. Since that time I have thought she used Africa and flirtation as a means to avoid what she had to do. Ducking what she had to do was a "flinch." She flinched, and she never copped to it. At the moment she was going to do this acting training, she decided to do something else. Instead of facing something in her training, her talent, her career, she flinched. She backed off. She went to Africa.

Flinch means to back off. To retreat. To lose courage. I say be there, make your choice, and don't flinch. Don't go to Africa for the wrong reasons. Flinching makes you less in charge, less the helmsman, less determining. When you flinch, you lose the opportunity, and in the process you sacrifice some determining part of you.

Flinching probably starts with some kind of confusion, some kind of a funny feeling like, "Can I do it?" Doubt. Fear. Retreat. Flinch. Then blame. And by then you're down at the bottom. So if you find yourself blaming your agent, your boss, your mother, your spouse, you know something's wrong back at the ranch. But what's wrong is not others, it's you. Again, Webster's:

FLINCH: To give way.

That would be enough. To give way.

Draw back. Yield ground in a combat. To turn aside from a course of action, a duty, or enterprise.

Unbelievable, isn't it? I'm big on numbers. I would say that 50 percent of all career problems are a result of flinching. Who doesn't have a good dream? Who doesn't have a good dream hidden somewhere that flinching hasn't deflected? Get that dream out of hiding. Then instead of ducking, get it going, make it known. Many unrealized dreams, good ones, lie somewhere in the cellar, molding, which is why writers make so much money writing about dreams.

To draw back through failure in courage, endurance, or resolve. To shrink from something as dangerous, painful, or difficult. To waver, deviate, be deflected. To slink, sneak off. To withdraw from, and lose one's ground.

And by the way, flinching is not just a quiet, passive activity. Some people flinch with anger, some flinch with grief, all flinch with justification. They declare they have good reasons not to do this or that. There are all kinds of dramatizations in flinching. You can flinch by blowing up at somebody and in this way avoid doing what you know you should do.

So it's got all this pullback stuff. To me, this quote

from the *Oxford English Dictionary* definition is quintessential:

> *"This flinching of his and absenting himself."*
> —Holland

In other words, when you flinch you become absent. You are no longer there. So how can you accomplish anything when you're not there? You're flinching. You're off your course. Flinching has to do with escaping. You flinch to get out. You flinch to get away from duty. You flinch to avoid confronting yourself and your dreams.

We have voices within us that weren't invented today. Demons have been mentioned all through history. Inner voices whispering doubts or shouting advice, often strange, destructive counsel. There are also voices from without. Even from people who love us. Some of this advice is constructive, friendly, and helpful. Take it. On the other hand, there is the debilitating, destructive symphony conducted by the dissonant, overzealous, negative doubter of all achievement: the fearmonger.

Everybody faces these voices, inner and outer, helpful and undermining. Every time I go to paint, I take the brush and right away I hear this voice of a family member who's also an artist saying, "You're about to spoil it. Let it go now. It's fine as it is. Don't put that green there. No more green. No! No! Don't do it!"

Every time I go to paint I hear this kind of advice. What I do is nod very quietly, firmly, and simply go on. I don't flinch. I do my work.

It's like sweeping an alley with a broom. You have a job to do, do it. Sweep the alley. Then, from the first-floor window, Mrs. Goldberg sticks her head out. "Vat's dat, vat are you doink down there? Vat are you fixink with dat little bristle? Vat's dat you're doink with a broom? You can't clean no alley with dat broom. Dat broom is a small broom. Take you two year to do dat alley." I say that you nod and go on. Then from the other side Mrs. Papadopoulos appears. "Hey, you bum. Τῆ κᾴνησ εκεὶ. Μη τό καθαρὶζησ βρε μᾴγγα. Φὶγαι! Git outta dere!" Nod and go on. But you better go on pretty fast. Because if you don't go on fast, and you start to get into a little discussion, look out. Did you ever talk to one of those ladies? You will not get out. You will not survive. You'll lose your pants, your jacket, your watch, your virginity, and eventually your mind. So don't get into a discussion. Keep sweeping the alley. If you don't, that's a flinch.

I think these inner and outer voices can interrupt you at every step of life. When talking to your boss, when calling the person who is always late paying their bills, when speaking to your landlord, when relating to your boyfriend, girlfriend, mother, father, business associate, whomever. Don't be swayed from your purpose. Don't flinch, just sweep.

One important thing I've found helpful: These inner

or outer voices, these people in the alley, they are not enemies. When you start creating the feeling that these people are enemies, it's immediately a battle. A battle you can lose. They're not the enemy, just misguided souls trying to help. And I wouldn't even tell them they were misguided. I'd just say, "Thanks a lot." Or better yet, just nod. You can still function while hearing the negative comments. You can still make your phone calls, you can still paint, you can still write, you can still operate. You will hear the noise diminish without doing anything more than just continuing to work. To do. Your way, at your pace. Sweep, sweep, sweep.

EXERCISE

1) Name three occasions in the past where you know you flinched.

2) What are you flinching from right now? Something on your to-do list that you're avoiding, some person, some action to advance your career? State what these items are and make your plans for executing them.

TERRORIST THEATER: GETTING IT DONE

In my acting class, I put an actress on Terrorist Theater. She wasn't working professionally, didn't have an agent, and though she had improved as an actress in class, she wasn't living up to her potential. I felt she still had the problem I had spotted in the first scene she did in class two years before, namely, she didn't believe she was an actress. I gave her a six-week ultimatum: Get a paying job as an actress, or you're out of class. That's Terrorist Theater.

The objective is to push actors through a stuck period in their careers where they are not fulfilling their potential. This drastic action is not taken indiscriminately. It's tough, but done with forethought and applied to the right person at the right time with love and care, it works. Once again, this principle, taken specifically in relation to acting, applies to all jobs and all careers. The principles underlying Terrorist Theater help make the person become a pro. You don't say, "I can't do it, they'll never hire me. I don't have enough experience." You don't say, "I can't get to the head of the firm." You don't say, "I can't get this report done by the deadline." You get it done within the deadline one way or another. That's being a pro.

In my classes, we have found that actors who went through Terrorist Theater have experienced something equivalent to priming an engine—a direct shot of fuel right into the cylinder. Their psychology? Bypassed. Negativity? Ignored. Fear? No time for it. Doubts? Forget them. They were forced to move, to act, to chase, to innovate, to hustle—all because the stakes were raised. Love the class? Get a job, or you're out. Permanently. The level of activity toward their careers exploded, such that we have a 75 percent success rate with those assigned to Terrorist Theater. They cared a great deal about the class and believed it was an essential tool to fulfill their careers. The threat of losing something they really valued increased their necessity to a much higher level. They pushed through. They got jobs.

Anyone in any field can understand and apply this principle. It can be used in a stuck period or as standard operating procedure. Raise the stakes. No excuses. Go for what you want. Demand more of yourself. You're capable of a great deal more than you imagine. You'll be amazed at how creative, energetic, and effective you can be.

The major hurdle in being a professional still remains getting the job, and then getting the job done. Totally. With excellence. No holds barred. I call it being an "artistic killer." Killing in the positive, creative sense— finishing what you started in the most glorious way. Don't say you tried. They don't pay for trying. It's when you push yourself to completion, no matter how high the stakes, that your full abilities come to life.

EXERCISE

1) Recall three deadlines you didn't meet. If the tasks were never finished and it is still appropriate to do so, finish them now.

2) Decide on three difficult current tasks, and make plans to get them done in a set period of time. Note them below, and as you complete each task, check it off.

_____ a. _____

_____ b. _____

_____ c. _____

CELEBRATE

If you're climbing a mountain, one of those Himalayan jobs, and you get up to 1,500 feet, celebrate. Have a little extra hot tea and a cookie. Don't look up at the 17,000 feet yet to go. It will discourage you. It may even cause you alarm. Just quietly celebrate and start up again after a good night's rest. This celebration is crucial, not just because it's encouraging but because it builds confidence and acts as a simple way of charting your progress.

Your career is not one big trek. It's a series of small, deliberate steps, punctuated by small celebrations. Later, as the victories become bigger, so do the celebrations. When you get to the top of the mountain, you can herald your victory with a real blowout tango in Paris. We need these signals, these markings, these commemorations of our progress. Take advantage of the opportunities to sing out your accomplishments as you head for the huzzahs.

EXERCISE

Pick out three of your victories from the last three years. If you haven't celebrated them, do so now. Indicate how you will make plans for future celebrations.

JEWELS OF THE NILE

Many act as if they were the jewels of the Nile. Perfect. As if every feather, every facet, every follicle were immaculate. Glistening. They feel if they were to change one tiny detail, the pyramids would crumble, the Nile would dry up. Well, that's not the way. This phony idea that we're complete as we are, stuck in this mold of perfection, in no need of any change, is a lie. There is no growth without change, and there is no career without growth.

I think it's important to give up something. Something about yourself. Something within. Something real. Like the idea that you are a certain kind of person who does things only one way, and that's the way you do it and you won't change for anybody. In order to grow, you need to sacrifice some stubborn, sticky idea about your pride, which is maintaining your dignity at the expense of getting things done. But what if you gave up this idea and changed? What if you became more viable, more open, more daring, more receptive, more effective? To have a free-flowing, developing career you need to be flexible in order to easily respond and take advantage of any opportunity. So c'mon, give something up, some gummy part of your make-up that's holding you back.

In working with an actress early on in a project, she

told me she was discouraged, frustrated with how the work was going. I said, "You're spoiled, aren't you?"

She said, "Yes. My parents did it."

I replied, "I know, I know. And you fought them every step of the way. Do you get that way with men?"

She said, "Yes."

"What about with your acting career?"

"No . . . well, yes."

"And what about the weather not being what you want?"

"Oh, no," she said. Then after a pause, "Yes, I do that, too."

"So this spoiled thing gets you in every area of your life."

"Yes."

"Spoiled means you always get your way or else you become unhappy and frustrated. You just whine and complain, and worst of all become a martyr. Even the weather is being done to you. Spoiled will lead you to all the negative aspects of your dreams: unreal, hazy, flimsy utopias where you whine, 'I wannit now, and easy, or I'll just throw it away.' Don't let this spoiled thing keep you from doing the tough things. It's dreams into action, not dreams into fantasyland and then fantasyland into nothing. No. Pick dreams that are doable and then accomplish them and strengthen yourself as a result. And then do the next one and the next and the next and so it opens out. You'll eventually get all that you want, even the seemingly impossible ones, and more. But you, as a spoiled person, pick the one you can't get, so that when you can't get it you can go back to that same old paisley blanket, lying on your bed weeping because of what they didn't give you. 'They don't understand me!' That lament is exhausting. Pick things you know you can accomplish. Got it?" She agreed, and on the spot began to write a long-delayed letter to a producer she wanted to work with.

To understand what is necessary to develop and change our ways, we need to know how to break the patterns, the habits of our lives. Most people don't know that what they are doing is a habit. In a sense, habit determines who you are and how you live. That is, who you are physically and emotionally. People define you by the way you do things. Habits administer your life.

1904 Webster's:

HABIT: A tendency or aptitude acquired by custom or frequent repetition.

Habit is a choice, one that you often don't know you've made. It can be a choice of physical appearance and behavior, or it can be a choice of attitude—perhaps one of those "character traits" that you feel is one of your untouchable jewels.

I was nine when I first heard the phrase "Know thyself." Little did I know how difficult and extensive this concept was and how inexorably tied to my career it would become. "Know thyself" through the years became not some form of ethereal search for the saintly me, but a practical look at what changes could have a positive effect professionally. One of the most difficult things I've faced is that change is possible. I think most of us would prefer that it remained impossible. It would be a relief not to have to confront the inherent difficulty of changing. "People don't change" is a sad, oft-recurring refrain that when sung drowns out the possibilities.

Change is one of the toughest paths you'll traverse, but with honesty and hard work, you'll see that your character is something you can develop and is not an invariable given to you at birth. To say this kind of personal work is difficult is a vast understatement, but you can, with persistence, make real changes. Now, I've seen jewelers cut, and I know that as tough as it is to create a flawless diamond from a rough stone, it's a piece of cake next to changing ourselves and our habits. Your way, your approach, the support you seek in this personal investigation is based on your personal choice. But do realize that this process of change must be done one way or another, because it is the most important journey you will face and can add immeasurably to your progress.

Throughout the world there are many deep-rooted and affecting habits, and to some of these we even assign the word *addiction*. I have often said that everyone is an alcoholic about something. Some about food, others about drugs, others about relationships. I'm not trying to bring these complex matters down to a simple equation, but once you're aware of a habit, and of the depth to which you're addicted to it, then you are in a position to stop it. Habit is mostly automatic, which in essence removes you from the action. You're not actually doing it, it's just happening to you. When you become aware, you are then breaking the automatic and putting yourself in control.

A willingness and ability to look at your habits will inevitably bring you to a place where you see them as your choices. No matter what the habits, they are to some degree your choice. And when you come to this understanding, you are more able to change or eliminate them. Kazantzakis, the celebrated author of *Zorba the Greek,* said that if you want to stop smoking, throw the cigarette away. The remarkable teacher from India, Krishnamurti, said that transformation, real change, happens now, in this instant. I wholeheartedly agree with both, and I believe this ability to change in the moment is a real key to your success.

As a businessman, if you tend to daydream during the weekly office meeting, that's a habit that needs changing. As an actor, if you tend to be ill-prepared for an audition, that's a habit that needs changing. If you tend to flinch, that's an evading, hiding habit that you've got to change. If you bring apathy, worry, false pride, self-centeredness, or bad vibes to a friendship on a fairly consistent basis, that's a habit that needs changing. If you go promiscuously from one relationship to another, never solving the problems in front of you, never fully committing yourself, this can be a whopper of a bad habit in life and definitely needs changing. If you're consistently down about your work, always feeling you've made no progress, showing your co-workers a sour puss with never a hint of enthusiasm, by all that is held holy, change that mother-grabbin' habit!

Many of the character traits we cling to as cornerstones are weak choices that prevent us from revealing our true selves and achieving what we want in our careers. Clutching to this stubborn, perfect definition of the so-called essential me is for the birds. So as you can see, from my point of view, *Dreams Into Action* is as much about you as it is about your dreams. It's about you in the sense that the smarter you are, the more open you are; the more focused you are, the more all becomes possible.

So, unfortunately, I have to repeat that change *is* possible. Habits can be broken, attitudes can evolve. Despite the difficulty, we all have to give up our concept that we are perfect jewels of the Nile. There's a better you right around the corner.

EXERCISE

Write down five habits you need to change. These can be habits of mind, body, or character. Change them, using the techniques of awareness and control discussed above.

Paint Your Own Portrait

Many people go through life apologizing for who they are, as if asking permission for their existence. Hiding, they travel along with an opaque, general, anonymous face. Or they pretend to be on their best behavior, as if that's going to win points. Well, it's not going to work. Who wants to work with somebody who comes into the office apologizing? Hiding? Who wants to live with the lover who utters the ever-deadening martyred lament, "Oh, no, everything is fine"? I can hear another mentor, Boris Aronson, the great theater designer, say, "A little cheerfulness wouldn't hurt."

If you're laying on a heavy dose of sucrose politeness, you're painting your portrait in a sickly candy pink. If you're filled with hostility and blame, you've got dark, dowdy, black-gray. If you're hiding and fearful to speak up, you've got screechy, unpleasant yellow and you're painting with a very limited, self-pitying palette. When you paint your portrait, load your brush with a lot of colors. Hot, bright colors. Or beautiful, soft pastels. Your choice. Just paint so that *you* sing out.

Recently my assistant was on the phone, talking to the framers for a painting exhibition of mine. We needed eight frames done two weeks earlier than we had agreed. My assistant's side of the conversation, which I overheard, went something like this: "Uh-huh . . . oh,

yeah . . . right . . . but, oh . . . uh-huh . . . right, okay. . . ."
Then he hung up. I said, "Well?" He said, "They can't."
I told him his part was not very exciting. His lines, which,
of course, he was writing, were dull and not colorful. His
was not a part Marlon Brando would want to play. And
on top of all that, he didn't get what he wanted.

I called the framers and asked, "How do you say
'please' in German?" They said, "Oh, no you don't!
Don't pull that on us!" I said, "Really. I just want to
know. Come on." They finally said, *"Bitte."* I said, with
warm, rose-colored charm, *"Bitte. Bitte.* Can you do at
least six?" They said they would think about it. The
next day I sent a package of lox and bagels with
"Bitte" written on the package. The frames were deliv-
ered one day earlier than we needed them.

In day-to-day life, there's a color for each moment
and mood—tough, sweet, charming, angry, enthusiastic,
sexy, witty—and an infinite variety of hues and shades to
deal with each situation that makes you alive and vivid.
As my dear friend James Leo Herlihy wrote, "Don't
look for a lover. Be one." So whether it's with your wife,
husband, mother, boss, business associate, lover, friend,
or accountant: Paint. Paint and give life all you've got.

EXERCISE

Name five areas where you can improve your portrait.
State specifically those new attitudes with which you will
now be painting.

GOOD MOVES

Take some time now to write down how you got to where you are. Be as specific as possible. What do you feel good about having accomplished? How did you achieve it? Go step by step, and don't miss a detail. You may have started drinking a protein drink every morning when things began to improve. Don't leave that seemingly minor detail out—it may be the ticket.

When things are going well, note your victories. What did you do to cause the good? Do more of that. Look back on your successes and analyze what you did to get there. The actions may be very diverse. You started making more phone calls, you gave up watching TV all the time, you gave up sugar and junk food, you took a much-needed vacation. Get it all down so that you understand what past actions made you feel good and caused good things to happen for you.

EXERCISE

1) Write down five successful actions from the past that you are no longer doing. Do them.

2) Come up with five new good moves. Do them.

LEVITY SOMETIMES NECESSARY WHEN TALKING TO ROCK

The following is a discussion on priorities I had with an actor in one of my classes.

STUDENT: I wonder if you could help me with a problem.

MILTON: *(In an exaggerated Charlie Chan Chinese accent.)* Problem? Most unusual. Actors never come to studio with problem.

STUDENT: Actually, it has to do with my parents. . . .

MILTON: Oh! Actor with family problem? Even more unusual. But more important for Number-One Son, what is with career? Developing along lines discussed in acting class?

STUDENT: I'm spending more time on my photography lately.

MILTON: Oh, photography! Excellent profession. Any other career Number-One

Son trying to cultivate simultaneously?

STUDENT: My father still hopes I'll become a lawyer. . . .

MILTON: So that's a wrap. End of discussion. Listen to father. Always good in Chinese tradition. Relieve guilt. Help father. Become lawyer.

STUDENT: But I want to be an actor! What is this Chinese bit?

MILTON: Of no great consequence. Developed while waiting for actors to make up minds. Patience necessary. So, acting, too? Now more complex. Photography. Lawyer. Acting. Have any other interests you would like to inform class of?

STUDENT: No . . . I mean, I wait tables to pay the rent.

MILTON: Understand. Waiter not great profession for you. Other interests?

STUDENT: Well, I ride horses. I do a little amateur rodeo.

MILTON: So want to be rodeo rider, too?

STUDENT: Part-time.

MILTON: Yes. Very good. Part-time is all of life. So, photography, lawyer, actor, unwanted profession of waiter, and rodeo rider part-time. Can these interests be focused into one energy?

STUDENT: That's my problem.

MILTON: Cannot make decision?

STUDENT: I have trouble with decisions.

MILTON: According to honorable Robert Bly, making decisions most necessary to becoming a man, a full person, a warrior.

STUDENT: I'd be giving up something if I choose just one.

MILTON: Necessary to give up many things. Necessary to give up ass in order to get to proper destination on journey. Bumpy ride on donkey or camel. Ass become very sore before arrival.

STUDENT: Are you telling me I should give these other things up and just concentrate on the acting?

MILTON: Oh no! Much better, young and oh-so-wise one, to plummet in all directions, crashing into walls of six different varieties, dispersing self all over landscape.

STUDENT: Can you be serious a moment? This is important.

MILTON: Levity sometimes necessary when talking to rock.

STUDENT: Rock? I'm not a rock. And you're not Chinese.

MILTON: Oh, that not true! I very much Chinese deep at roots. Maybe everyone is. China oldest and wisest of cultures. Now back to rock. You have to somehow make decision. Which profession? Focus on it. Resolve situation.

STUDENT: All right. Enough already. I want to be an actor. I think.

MILTON: Oh, actor! I thought was going to be

rodeo rider. Maybe decision should be based on most beautiful women. Many pretty women in rodeo. Yes? Rodeo rider very attractive. Yes? Especially if bareback. But wait moment. Kim Basinger, Julia Roberts, Michelle Pfeiffer not in rodeo. So, on second thought, maybe better idea to be actor.

STUDENT: Does every decision have to come down to whether or not we get sex out of it?

(A pause ensues, as Milton grins coyly.)

MILTON: Confucius say, "Not necessary to answer obvious question."

STUDENT: How do I make a decision? How do I choose?

MILTON: Put down on paper all professions. Follow linkage. Connect with what you want. Seek out ideal profession to ideal conclusion. Find one most attractive. One most fulfilling to you. Your dream. Your destiny. Take time. Gestate. Then, with godlike wisdom, make selection. Then, please, pursue.

STUDENT: So when I make a choice, I'll have more clarity?

MILTON: Necessary first to find choice. To make selection. On paper. Define priority. Then focus. Execute. Deliver. A thousand thanks for your great patience. This discussion has presented many clues to your eventual downfall. Just making little Chinese joke.

EXERCISE

Write down your interests and avocations. Prioritize and give the appropriate amount of time to each. You won't be the first person to have your hobby become a major part of your career.

Horrors!

"**I** am going to fail. I will not make it. I am not enough. My career is over." Aren't we fascinated by the spectre of not succeeding? Isn't failure fascinating? Isn't it compelling? In a sort of sick way, we are seduced, almost hypnotized, by our grotesque fear of failure.

The other side of this compulsion is denial. Sometimes things are not as we want them, but we pretend they are and go on, almost celebrating as if all were well. Remember in those horror movies how the villagers were always dancing in the town square just before the monster appears? They know the monster is in the vicinity. It's been spotted. They've been warned by the scientist to be on the alert. But they blithely dance on. Your monster is failure, and as it lumbers ever closer, you are either stopped in your tracks, feverishly possessed and mesmerized by the beast of doom, or you are dancing the villagers' glib dance, pretending it doesn't exist.

As addictive as the drama of failure can be, you've got to let it go. Let the monster do its thing, you do yours. Don't just stand in awe, fascinated by its terrifying hulk. If you do, it could crush you. Remember, it is your career monster. Its intent is to stop you. It spreads its evil odor of doubt to wreak havoc with your career. Don't stick around, waiting to be engulfed in a passive paralysis. Move. You can outfox it with small, deliberate actions. Simple things. These are the real deterrents that will transform your monster into a benign, almost sweet Godzilla. Reorganize your desk, pay your bills, answer those letters, make calls to set up your appointments, do your budget. Write out the specific problems you're having and execute more precise plans to resolve them. All of these simple actions are therapeutic, but they will also tame the monster within and get you onto the positive side of your career, opening up your future.

EXERCISE

State specifically what doubts you have, and what precise tasks you will now execute to abate these fears.

BLAME HEAVEN

Get that spotlight off me! I don't want to look at myself. I didn't do anything. Why shine it on me? My boss. That's right, my boss. Yeah, him. Let's shine it on him. It's his fault. That's better. Let's also shine that light on my mother. Oh, yeah, my mother. She's a part of it. God knows, a big part. Ah, that's better. She deserves that light on her. And my wife. Oh, yeah. My wife. She's always doing me in. Shine it on her. That's good! Okay! That feels much better. And as long as we're at it, let's shine that spotlight on my kids. They're always at fault. Distracting me. Better. Much better.

Oh, and another thing . . . I don't think I ever told you about the terrible things that have happened to me. If I have, let me tell you again. Once upon a time I was abused as a child. I was hit when I was a kid. I was thrown off the team as a teenager. I flunked out of college as a young adult. And now, as a maturing person, my marriage is on the rocks. Pain. Sorrow. Regret. Others did it to me. Boy, did they ever. Without any real reason, they attacked me, acted against me, and they—I'm talking "they" with a capital T—THEY did me in. Good! Now I can go on with my life—as fraught with tragedy as it is—

and know that it's what others have done to me that
makes me what I am. Amen.

To have a career culminate in the realization of
your dreams, you must embrace the reality that you,
and only you, run your life. No one else can cause you
to fail, falter, or abide by their wishes. It's your script,
your movie. When you blame others, you're allowing
other writers to change your best lines, alter entire
scenes in your masterpiece. After thirty years of help-
ing people confront their careers, I can say with
certainty that the most pernicious deterrent to
advancement is the victim mentality. Blame creates
victims.

Nothing destroys people but themselves. You've
got to believe that. Otherwise, you go around blaming
all kinds of things: your parents, the business, the
weather, your relationships, your parents, your horo-
scope, your parents, your childhood, your adulthood,
your parents, the national deficit, the government,
inflation, the younger generation, Bush, Clinton,
Reagan, Lincoln, Washington, and, oh yes, your parents. Nonsense. It's you. It's in your hands.

No one can do anything to you unless you agree to
let them. It only happens with your approval. It takes
two to tango. The "They did it to me!" way of thinking
leads you—bags packed, passport stamped, and passage booked—to Blame Heaven, where everyone sits
around blissfully blaming. Where it's so overcrowded

that they're gouging the tenants with exorbitant rents for studio apartments without a view.

Blame is seductive. If you're an actor, when an agent doesn't submit you and you don't get a shot at winning the part, very subtly, with real justification, you feel he has done you in. Oh yeah, the agent did it. Sounds good. Feels good. When it feels this good you can know for sure you are solidly in the seductive embrace of blame.

The truth is the last time you met with your agent you had an argument you failed to resolve. But that doesn't pop into your thoughts. More than that, you forgot that you didn't even respond to your agent's last two phone calls. But this doesn't occur to you, either. By omitting these episodes, you, under the influence of blame, are rewriting your own history. These omissions are tantamount to a lie. You can't see or recall them because you don't dare face your own music.

BLAME: To find fault. To accuse. To rebuke.

In the court of victimhood, the plaintiff seeks redress and desperately tries to pin culpability on the accused. What we want is the other person wrong and me right at any cost. Blame is a false accusation made in a feeble attempt to defray the guilt of one's own failure. Blame may feel self-righteously good for a brief moment. Then it fades, leaving you worse off than before. Like chocolate or sugar taken in times of stress, blame provides soothing temporary relief, a rush that soon crashes into a deflating letdown.

As you read this, you might find your own case to be an exception. You believe you have *real* justification in your specific scenario. Yours is some special circumstance not covered by this chapter. "I'm not blaming, but ..." can be a clever attempt to escape the truth, but only that. An attempt. Blame is self-justifying, so look more closely. There's something you've done or something you've been remiss in carrying out, either of which has contributed to this difficult situation. No matter what you may think the other person did to you, you have to look at your part, your responsibility—what you brought to the party.

> *BLAME: To assign cause to others, thereby making others more powerful than you.*

When you blame, you sign off the rights to your life. Others are running your show and you are powerless to stop them. When you point the finger, you are saying, "He is stronger and therefore ruling me. I can't do it my way because he's ruling the roost, taking the play away." If your parents don't agree that you will be a smash hit, you blame them for your inability to go forward, and claim they are holding you back. You empower them to rule over your life. You are less. They are more.

BLAME: To blaspheme. To censure. To discredit.

The root of the word *blame* is from the Greek *blásphemos:* to blaspheme, to speak irreverently, to slander or abuse. Self-blame would be the worst kind of abuse. Self-blame, or any blame, is not responsibility. Responsibility does not seek who's wrong. Blame is all about nailing who's wrong. Responsibility does not attack anyone. Blame is a blasphemous attack on someone. Responsibility is simply saying, "This is what I did to bring about what happened, and here's what will set it right."

We eagerly sit around yakking up blame. Let me state it plainly: We just *love* to blame. It's compelling. The universal song. The world sings out blame with you in five-billion-part harmony. It's one of the main gigs in all human relationships—personal, business, or political. Seemingly innocent complaints will be sympathetically encouraged and supported by most. "Oh, you poor dear! How do you endure it?" And on and on goes the beat.

Do you have accomplices in the blame game? When you complain about what someone else did to you, do some of your friends eagerly rush in to agree? These are not real friends. A real friend would say, "Will you cut this blame crap and quit complaining about what they did to you? What did you do? What can you do to fix it?" That's what an honest friend will do for you.

COMPLAIN: To grieve. To murmur. To grumble. To find fault.

Finding fault. Sound familiar? It's clear that complaining, bitching, grumbling, and murmuring are just more disguises for seductive, subtle, insidious blame. Such sullen discontent is either on the road to or has already arrived in Blame Heaven. This grumbling fuels your passage and ignites the pleasant glow of the lamp by your bedside upon arrival.

Without blame present, you have the idea to visit your boss, discuss your contributions, and ask for a much-needed raise. He agrees and you walk out more aligned with him and with a better salary for your family. With blame, you never even think to meet with the boss, you never talk to him, you become even more angry at him because he's a tyrant who keeps you from progressing. You wind up in the cafeteria, dishing the dirt with your blame soulmate.

So let me give it to you unvarnished: Blame is rotten. It disempowers you. It fuels conflict. It feeds your monster of doom and justifies your "inability" to execute actions that will carry you forward in your career. From walking to the invention of the wheel, from the horse to the stagecoach, from the flivver to the Ferrari, the means of locomotion have varied all through the ages, but the wayward destination for those who would fail to accomplish their dream remains the same: Blame Heaven.

EXERCISE

Name five times you blamed someone, and note how the blaming held you back.

BLAME: THE CURE

If someone is throwing stones in your path, it doesn't mean you have to become a chump, a dupe, a helpless fall guy. A chump has a tough time making his or her career sail. If the neighbor's sprinkler is spraying your car, walk over and have a talk with him. Make some adjustments to the aim of the nozzle. Don't wait until your car's paint job is ruined. Don't threaten expensive lawsuits. Don't sit around complaining about what a jerk he is for letting the sprinkler wander onto your drive. Walk over and deal with him. Don't be a victim stewing in the juice. Just fix it.

Blame can be sadly noble. At home, you might say to your kids, "Try as I may to support this family and give you what you need, I'm not given the chance to work on what I hold dear. It's always so damn noisy!" Hey, baby, it's your house, fix it. Don't blame the kids. Fix it. Get a studio outside of the house and work all you want. For three hours of the day, or however long you need, have the rest of the family fend for themselves.

If you find yourself in your relationships weary of having to patch things up after a fight, of having to initiate a talk to smooth things out—if over and over again you are the one to fix things, and it all seems a wearisome burden—be aware that you are seeking a payback for all your trouble, hardship, and effort.

Each time you fixed it you felt this weariness because you were working so hard to "do good." It became a tough chore. Nothing wears you out faster than laboring to "do good."

Actually, with each bit of your so-called help, you were setting up the other person for blame down the line. In other words, you weren't simply offering to fix it, you were also building up resentment. "Here I go again, always the one who fixes." You lie in wait, lurking in the bushes for one too many exhausting fixes, until you fall on the other person with an avalanche of blame. "Why me? Why is it always me who fixes?" Oh, weary, weary. No wonder you're tired. When you decide to fix it, it should be light, pleasurable, a way of life, a blessed action.

It may sound funny to you, but when you speak to your neighbor about his sprinkler, you might start with, "Wow, this is one of the strongest sprays I've ever seen, and your lawn really looks great." You'll find he's much more receptive. Then begin to tell him about the problem of your car getting wet. This praise may seem minimal, but it maximizes your chance of fixing the problem. Praise has made your job much easier. Try it, you may like it: When blame rears its ugly head, think and give praise instead.

Do I hear a voice of protest? "Wait a minute! I've gone along with you up till now, and let me tell you it's been pretty damn difficult. But you're trying to tell me that if some bastard has done me in, I should offer praise in return? *Ha!* That's right, I say *Ha!*" Difficult, isn't it? I have to admit it is damn near impossible. The voice of protest is at times my own. When you are feeling done in, to offer praise is as unheard of as being slapped in the face and saying in response, "That was a good smack." Turning the other cheek is not what this is about. This is about knowing that when you feel someone has done you harm, before you hurl insults, look at what you did and think about offering praise instead.

Look for something positive to extend to the other person. If you are an actor and a director is not providing what you need, first try approaching her with some credit for something she's done that helped you. Now when you ask her for what you need, she's in a much better frame of mind to provide it. The know-how of making your point in a constructive manner that avoids the other person feeling put down is one of the important steps in the dance of life.

PRAISE: To honor. To prize. Glorify. Esteem.

In my experience, the world neither offers nor accepts praise easily. "If I offer praise, will it be perceived as a weakness in my character? Do I lose my advantage? Will I lose the aggression that I need to win? Will I appear phony if I extend it? Phony if I accept it?" We are suspicious of praise as the first tentative steps toward intimacy. Are we letting them get too close?

A human being is trying in his way to have a mean-ingful life, to be creative, to fight the good fight, to do art, to employ commerce, to engage in politics, to love, to be loved, to sing. He is striving all his days to become the best he can be. Praise is a simple acknowl-edgment of a job well done, and a gentle encourage-ment that he go on. I think it's a good idea to let him or her know before they're gone.

I'm not suggesting that in the midst of conflict this will be easy to accomplish. Nor do I advocate solutions suitable only for those who dwell in the rarefied atmos-phere of the hallowed saint. Praise is a spiritual action that will reward you in many ways, including your being more effective. But be patient. Don't beat your-self up with this concept. At first, just try to notice the difference between the old way and the new. I'm advo-cating practical, useful ways to shift from being at the mercy of blame to becoming the cause of a solution.

> *"There is a magic formula for resolving conflict: Have as your objective the resolution of the conflict, not the gaining of advantage."*
> —Peace Pilgrim, American traveler

So this new, bright-as-a-penny choice goes down like this: The next time blame threatens to sneak up on you, try a compliment instead of a rebuke, encourage-ment rather than a black eye. Offer praise in lieu of a lawsuit. Instead of muttering and complaining, offer a clear, easily received, constructive solution. A friendlier time for all. Be kind to yourself as well as to others. The bleak alternative is, as Macbeth says, to let "tomorrow, and tomorrow, and tomorrow creep in this petty pace from day to day," allowing blame, bitterness, alienation, and recrimination—the old ways—to rule the roost.

With all my heart I pray that you and I have the courage to take these bold steps so we can get along with each other and lead more enlightened lives.

EXERCISE

Take five situations where blame is involved, and use the techniques in this chapter, including praise, to resolve them.

SELF-ESTEEM: WHAT YOU DESERVE

What do you deserve? Many stumble through their lives as if they deserve life imprisonment rather than the pot of gold sitting at the end of the rainbow. There are other people who seem to be moving along smoothly—they've defined their dream, honed their concept, created a launching pad for activity, even begun aggressively to pursue their goal—but they're still crippled by the nagging attitude that they don't deserve the bounty they seek.

I had an interesting conversation with a friend who drives a real junker of a car. (I seem to be surrounded by people with terrible cars.) He says he can't wash it because of two broken windows, and until he fixes the windows (which he maintains he can't afford), he can't think about fixing the numerous other mechanical problems. The windows cost about $125 installed. This isn't the problem—he could dig up a hundred bucks if he needed it. I believe what actually is going on is a crash of concepts. A vision collision. One concept is that of a starving *artiste,* driving through the lean years with this vehicular embarrassment, this symbol of potential achievement not yet realized. The other is the concept of a successful actor in a hot car.

After I talked with him further, he confessed that

because he owed some money on credit cards, he thought of his car as a form of penance for the sins of previous irresponsibility. He defined himself as something of a loser, demonstrating through his possessions a struggling, downbeat status in life. He wanted better, but did nothing to improve the car.

To me, self-esteem is the only issue here. My call is that if he fixed the car, he would put himself in a more positive, creative frame of mind, and he would be able to make more money and pay off this debt faster. Had he already cast himself in the role of suffering *artiste*? Why? Didn't he feel he deserved more?

These questions elicited some real anger at his family. Some blame. Some spite. "Fine. You won't help me on my actor trip? No problem. I'll starve. I'll drive this junker. Maybe even have an accident because of the brakes. How'd you like that?" He was extremely emotional as he spoke.

Look around you right now. Look at your possessions. Look at your apartment. Is there dust everywhere? Unwashed dishes? A pile of laundry to be done? Do they exist because of an unappreciative family, an unjust society that doesn't recognize you for the genius you are? Or have you cast yourself as this suffering, undeserving person who must do penance? You deserve more than that. If you are diligent, hard working, essentially free from blame, and not stuck or dwelling in the past, then you deserve nothing but the best. The best career. The best car. The best apartment. The best clothes. Whatever you can dream up, you deserve it.

Keep in mind that in getting what you deserve, the issue is not always money. But it is always about self-esteem. I remember visiting a group of artists who had very little money, living in a house in not such a terrific neighborhood. But the place was immaculate. Clean. Each person had decorated his or her room to his or her own taste, some with Christmas lights, others with carefully chosen cloth from the thrift store, so that it became a place of inspiration rather than one of dread.

Those who have cleaned their apartment after letting it run down have experienced a sense of pride and even the sense of feeling better about their whole life. How many times have you purchased an old silver utensil, or a used piece of furniture, and by cleaning and polishing it, found that the object improves greatly? The rehabilitated object reflects your expertise, your character. When you change the object and make it shine, you've done the same for yourself.

When you serve penance for sins of the past, you only succeed in bringing that attitude with you wherever you go. If this penance is based on some feeling of "Oh, yeah? Well, go to hell!" then know you're only empowering those you curse at your own expense. Deserve the best. Demand it for yourself. And when you demand it, see how far your reach expands, how many possibilities present themselves.

EXERCISE

1) Clean your apartment. Reorder your possessions.

2) Name five items you own that need some attention, and state how you can improve their condition through repair or, if need be, replacement.

THE PROBLEM IS THE SOLUTION

An acquaintance of mine has a brother, thirty-odd years old, a brilliant violinist, who has never escaped the university. At twenty-two, he graduated from Harvard with a bachelor's degree in Chinese history, but he had a goal to pursue a violin career. However, he received an offer to serve as a resident tutor the following year and took them up on it. After all, it was only for a year. Four years later he gave up his post as resident tutor to pursue his violin career. But during the summer he decided that with only two or three years left on his doctorate in Chinese history, he'd stay and get that Ph.D. Four years later he got his Ph.D. and talked up a storm about finally pursuing his violin career. He went to China for a time and traveled, and even played the violin there, to a fair amount of notice. He came back. He went back to Harvard and took a junior teaching position in—what else?—Chinese history. I spoke with him once and he talked coolly and eloquently about how the problem of achieving his dream, the violin thing, was that each time he was ready to go with the music career, these great opportunities in academia would present themselves.

What I told him is what I'm about to tell you. The problem of getting all wrapped up in these academic opportunities is a solution. It's a solution to the *real* problem of this man facing up to his talent as a musician and letting the world see it. So check out your problems. What do they solve for you? What do they save you from facing? Got a problem? You don't have time to prepare for your bar exam? What's that a solution for? Does it solve having to face your talent as a lawyer? Or do you not have time to prepare that corporate presentation? Perhaps that solves having to confront the bigwigs and prove yourself. Got a "time" problem? Got a "money" problem? Got a "relationship" problem? What do these attention getters help you avoid? What deeper problems do these solve? In the end, as with our violinist friend, are these problems an answer to not having to test your talent with the possibility of failure?

If you're dealing with a situation where some "problem" stands between you and pursuing your dream, check it out. I asked my editor if he had any such problem, and after a bit he replied, "I can't take piano lessons as often as I'd like because I can't afford them."

I said, "Ah, money. Money is always one of the big ones. What does this money problem solve for you regarding these piano lessons?"

"It keeps me from having to practice so much each week to prepare."

"That's not it. You love hard work," I replied. He pondered for a moment.

"It keeps me from finding out how good I am?"

"Bingo. You have the same problem as the Harvard violinist. He will find these academic job offers presenting themselves endlessly in order to avoid facing the music, literally and figuratively. And you, you have this money thing where you can't 'afford' to discover the reaches of your talent. You both need to resolve the doubts, the fears, the actual problems that prevent you from facing the outside world with your music."

When I first went to New York to pursue my career, fresh from college, I had some very good jobs working as a "gofer" for some important directors. A gofer is a glorified errand runner—you go for coffee and occasionally take notes for the director. This was a great apprentice time for me, working with Elia Kazan, Josh Logan, and Sanford Meisner, but money was not coming in easily. I had to hustle at all kinds of jobs to make ends meet. You name it, I did it—from waiter to cab driver to dishwasher and more. The problem was that many of the jobs either took too much of my energy or conflicted time-wise with my gofer jobs. I also needed time for acting and directing auditions. Having tried every solution I could think of, it got to the point where I felt nothing would solve my problem.

As I was about to throw up my hands in exasperation, a friend mentioned to me that he worked for a moving company in Greenwich Village. I vividly remember meeting these wonderful guys, the movers, one cold morning on Christopher Street. It was so cold they invited me at 7:00 A.M. to have a drink to get warm. That morning we moved someone from the

Village to Central Park West. It was an all-day job, but the pay and tips were terrific. Although the work was tough, I liked it and found that it perfectly solved my problem. People usually move at the beginning and end of the month. So for eight days a month I was busy on the moving truck, and then I was free for the other three weeks to push my career. The money was good enough to support me for the month and there were fringe benefits as well. I learned about people's furnishings, personal objects, and eccentricities, all of which have helped me as a director. And I'll never forget the men who I worked with on the trucks—wonderful, warm, full-of-heart guys who enriched my life. So I solved my problem of supporting myself until my career got going, and in the bargain learned a great deal more about people.

From industrialist to artist, at the heart of every success story lies a person trying to solve problems. Tough ones. Real ones. Not personal problems, but creative problems connected to their work. They use their talents to solve these problems for the betterment of the world. W. Edwards Deming had a problem: how to bring Japan, an essentially toy manufacturing nation, into the broad, competitive market following World War II. Solution: a whole system for industrial management, including new relationships between management, labor, and consumer that turned Japan into the industrial force it is today. Pablo Picasso and Georges Braque had a problem: They were trying to break the rules of perspective in art that impressionism had upheld. Solution: cubism, a whole new movement in art history that opened the door to modernism in painting. Maya Angelou had a problem: African Americans and the conditions that led to their oppression were not fully understood. Solution: personal, passionate poetry that conveys, without blame, the pain and joy of being an African American, and so gets us all to understand more. Frank Lloyd Wright had a problem: He perceived that architecture was desecrating landscapes for the sake of new buildings. Solution: buildings such as Fallingwater that utilize landscape, weaving nature's design into the design of man. What makes an industrialist, artist, poet, architect, or person in any field great is the clarity with which he or she sees a problem in society, and the talent and passion exerted to resolve it.

You have to differentiate on the subject of problems—as you can see, there are different types. If it's a personal problem you're using to avoid another issue, know it, deal with it, and resolve it. If it's a real problem getting in the way of your career, confront it and study it carefully and you will find the solution. If it's a problem in the world at large that needs fixing, and it interests you, put all you have behind it and help society. Therefore, know the different kinds of problems, each with its own solution.

There is no scarcity of solutions. You are not limited to only one choice, regardless of how emotionally heavy you feel, and how heavily impossible things seem. Heavy, heavy, bogged down. Oh, lighten up! Be creative. Don't blow your soul on your problems. Treat your problems as friends. They are. They require resourceful, imaginative solutions. It takes courage and persistence to solve a problem. Each answer, each solution will give you more and more confidence. Use your problems, be inspired by them, unravel them, and create a career and a life through the challenge they present.

EXERCISE

Write down all the problems you are currently experiencing, and put them into the three categories discussed in this chapter:

1) Apparent problems you use to avoid getting what you actually want;

2) Practical problems you need to resolve to make things work more effectively;

3) Something in the outside world that needs solving, and you're the person to do it.

State what you can do with respect to each of these types of problems.

SCARCITY

Have you been in a relationship where you thought you were losing your companion, and you felt if you lost him or her the world would end? You had that feeling, usually an anguished, cramping discomfort in the stomach, that if you lost this person there would be no hope, there would be nothing but pain. Then an interesting phenomenon occurs. At the very moment when you say, "It's over, *fini,*" either the person comes back or another suddenly appears. Your ability to finish opens the door to a new beginning.

I'm not saying that if you treasure a relationship you shouldn't work strongly to salvage it. The struggle to make things right with someone you love is done to your fullest. But keep in mind that your relationships are a tightrope, a balancing act that constantly affects your career. So here's another thought, seemingly risky, for you to balance. There is no scarcity in this world. No scarcity of relationships, of talent, of jobs, of money, of love. No scarcity.

The idea of scarcity is produced by the inner terror within us that we will not be able to find more of what we've lost. The possibility of losing a relationship, a job, anything, frightens us into an emotional state of rigidity. We hurt. We freeze up. We panic. The potential loss acts as a huge rejection and we feel insecure and shattered.

There is an ever-present tyranny that people feel about the fear of being fired. Fear of being fired by your boss. Fired by your girlfriend. Fired by your family. This threat, this fear makes it impossible to function properly. A big sale is flubbed, petty fights occur, important appointments are missed, your attitude goes down the tubes. Muscles tighten, appetite lessens, the stomach cramps, our equilibrium is lost. It is difficult even to breathe, and sometimes even the desire to live leaves us. And all of this is just the *fear* of losing. We cling desperately to what we have because we feel that's all we're entitled to, and there's nothing else for us.

How many times have you seen a friend in trouble in a relationship, and thought, "Good, she's finally going to be rid of him. She'll do so much better." But she's just beside herself with this terrible loss. She feels she can't go on. Or you're acquainted with a couple who are going through a tough time. You know a wonderful, lighthearted, and fun-filled dinner, or a walk on the Santa Monica Pier, or a skate in Rockefeller Plaza would rescue this overly serious relationship. But it's not possible. They're so trapped by the fear of loss, they can't put any real lightness, real juice, real life into their shared, parched existence.

You must be free to function, free to create, whether in your job or in your personal relationships. Communicate to your boss or lover, freely and easily. Romance, by its sheer nature, needs to be lighthearted, fun, free spirited. Instead we are nervous, uptight, shut down. We can't do what we need to do to help the situation. The irony is that the fear of losing intimacy is what keeps us from gaining intimacy. Learn to turn it around. Don't be so uptight that you might lose your companion, but inventive enough to create the fun and whimsy that a relationship needs to flourish.

Pittsburgh. The late 1930s. Fear was rampant as to where the next meal would come from. There was little in the way of excitement, just the day-to-day struggle to make ends meet. Little or no surprise existed, and hope was at a low ebb. In the middle of this, a man sold his life insurance policy. He bought a new car, a fur coat for his wife, boxing gloves for his sons, and four full bags of groceries for the family. He drove up the street for the neighborhood to see. The celebration was deafening. That was my father, and he taught me this lesson in scarcity. I never forgot it. Thanks, George.

Let fear as a way of life come to an end. Fear keeps you from making the right moves. Fear makes you keep quiet about that new idea because, God forbid it doesn't work, you might lose your job. Fear keeps you clinging to destructive relationships as if they were your finest possession.

If you fear losing, you've already lost. Instead, be exhilarated by the possibilities and revel in your power. Hold yourself in the high esteem you deserve. In your relationships, even if you lose, don't collapse. There are innumerable ones yet to come where intimacy will flourish. In your work, even if you're fired, don't despair. There are other jobs where your value will be appreciated. Actually, there is abundance. *Abbondanza!* There are many, many opportunities, many possibilities. The idea of scarcity on this planet is a lie.

EXERCISE

1) List five things you're afraid to lose, and discover how this fear makes you less effective with regard to each.

2) Communicate to the people in these situations, and take the actions necessary to turn these conditions around.

TOUGH GUYS

MILTON: So what's going on with you?

ACTRESS: I just can't do it anymore. I've got a day job, I've got my two kids, and money is always a problem. It's zapping me and I'm sick of it.

MILTON: I see.

ACTRESS: I just have to give up on my acting.

MILTON: Is there anything else you can do? Anything we can talk about?

ACTRESS: *(Tearfully.)* Talk. Talk. No, I just can't.

MILTON: *(Imitating Humphrey Bogart.)* So it's a wrap, huh, sweetheart?

ACTRESS: *(Through her tears.)* What did you say?

MILTON: *(Bogie again.)* It's a wrap, baby cakes.

ACTRESS: That's the worst Bogie imitation I've ever heard.

MILTON: I do Charlie Chan much better. Would you like that?

ACTRESS: Stop it.

MILTON: I'll stop my Bogie if you stop your Joan Crawford martyr.

ACTRESS: Well, it just can't work, and I'm real sad. We have our mortgage payments, the kids' schooling, and all our other expenses.

MILTON: How about giving up the family estate?

ACTRESS: *(Tearfully.)* That's what we've worked so hard for. It's our dream.

MILTON: There's Crawford again, doll. Maybe you've got to give up one dream for another. Get out of Beverly Hills. Sell the big house and buy something smaller in the Hollywood flats. Talk to the family about it.

ACTRESS: I can't talk to the kids, they're just eight and eleven.

MILTON: They'll understand. Besides, you're try-
             ing to help them become what they can
             become, right?

ACTRESS: Of course.

MILTON: Then let them help you become all you
             can become. How about your husband?

ACTRESS: (*Crying again.*) I guess he's okay about
             my being an actress.

MILTON: (*Bogie again.*) You guess, sweetheart?

ACTRESS: Stop that! The truth is I don't know.

MILTON: Then you'd better find out.

ACTRESS: That's a real tough one. It just kills me.

MILTON: Sounds like that's the bottom line.

ACTRESS: I guess it is. I'm afraid.

MILTON: Of what?

ACTRESS: I'm afraid he's not for my acting. Or
             worse, he doesn't care.

MILTON: Find out. Now.

ACTRESS: *(Now mocking Joan Crawford.)* Oh no! Don't make me do it. Please, please.

MILTON: *(Bogie.)* If he's tough on you, pussycat, me and some of the boys will straighten him out.

ACTRESS: I guess you're right. I have to talk to him.

MILTON: Great. Then you'll know where you stand. One more thing . . .

ACTRESS: Don't tell me. I have to start selling my body.

MILTON: Close. You've got to give up your day job and get one that pays less but doesn't zap you so much.

ACTRESS: Our budget is already so tight.

MILTON: *(Bogie.)* Jeez, you stumped me there. Poor Joan.

ACTRESS: Damn you.

MILTON: Solve it.

ACTRESS: I can't. I can't.

MILTON: *(Intoning.)* Woe is me!

ACTRESS: Now what? Who was that?

MILTON: Barrymore.

ACTRESS: Oh no.

MILTON: Get it together. It just means getting another day job.

ACTRESS: All right. Okay. I'll get one. . . .

MILTON: Good. Talk to your husband and the kids. Let them all in on it, and maybe as a bonus, you'll all get closer together. *(Bogie.)* Sweetheart.

ACTRESS: Okay, okay. Anything is better than this awful Bogie you do.

MILTON: Talk about hurting someone's feelings.

(END OF DISCUSSION)

If you're married, living with someone, or part of a family, make sure you are all trying to support each other's individual careers. Or, if there's one goal that the whole family is working toward, focus on accomplishing that. In any case, don't get trapped into chasing and maintaining a lifestyle. The lifestyle thing, the money thing, the white-house-with-a-picket-fence thing. All the materialistic games that people play are such a rat race that you'll lose the dream in no time flat.

My editor told me a story that after his first week in Los Angeles, he went to get a haircut and the barber told him, "You've been here a week, huh? You better get on it. Get to doing what you want to do." He cut for a bit, then said, "I remember when I came out here, and now it's seventeen years later and I don't remember why I came." The dream is elusive, often like a shooting star, streaking across the sky and burning itself out a lot quicker than one would like.

Artists are masters of the "day job syndrome," keeping the rent paid, the body fed, all the bases covered through one job, while at the same time pursuing an entirely different, difficult, and time-consuming career. Actors are famous for this, but anyone who has a dream faces this juggling act, especially in today's economic quagmire.

Watch it. Do not allow the day job either to drain your energy or be used to answer the demand for too much lifestyle. Lifestyle is a killer. Lifestyle will masquerade as your dream realized. Soon, like the actress in the discussion above, the lifestyle will seem more important than the dream. Appearances, comforts, and keeping up with the Joneses is not the road to a full future. Again, stay lean and trim. Be tough. Get your career concept done. That's the deal.

EXERCISE

1) Note down how your attachment to lifestyle is draining energy from the pursuit of your dream. What can you give up?

2) Write out a clear, concise, realistic budget.

3) Ensure that in a relationship or family, you're being supported in your career goals. If not, resolve the situation.

ON CALL

In the entertainment field, the famous dictum is, "The show must go on." This not only serves as a professional ethic but is often the motto that saves people in "the Biz" from undue suffering in the wake of a disaster. There are many famous stories, many that I have observed, where actors have turned in brilliant performances under the most excruciating personal circumstances. Outside the arts, I've known office workers, factory workers, tailors, and builders who have gone to work while under duress or under the weather, and have not only completed the day's work but did some of their best work.

The world doesn't check on or care about the emotional or physical state you're in. It's true of firefighters, doctors, police officers, emergency relief workers. The call comes, and they've got to perform at their best. Everyone can learn from those professions where people are "on call." Actually, the truth is everyone is on call—at work and in their life.

Let's say you're an actor, and after preparing yourself for six years, you finally get a really good part. You're excited as hell. On the day you shoot your big scene with the star, your escrow doesn't close, your agent calls you on the set with a problem about your contract, one of the kids has come down with the mumps, and the muffler goes out on your car. Six years, and all this has to happen today. Well, it might, and usually does. You still have to shoot the scene and be sensational.

I broke my ankle once playing basketball, and shortly afterward decided to resume teaching. I remember the first night back, talking to actors and working on scenes while tears were welling up from the pain. I kept going. I felt great that I kept going. And I was able to finish the class. The lesson is not only one in professionalism but in finding the personal strength gained from working despite a crisis. The Russian author Leo Tolstoy said, "Adversity builds character."

Today's society invites us daily to indulge our justifications, indulge our psychology, indulge in the reasons why we can't get the job done right. I find this trend simply unethical. Everyone is under duress. We as individuals must deal with life's endless trials and tribulations in a manner that does not deter us from either our immediate purpose or our long-range plans. The modus operandi of life is that we are on call. On call to work effectively, drive safely, cook happily, entertain like Auntie Mame, and be ready at all times with a professional attitude. Be a professional. A professional won't waste his or her life or impede his or her own career. A professional will prove his or her worth. Once, in the middle of a divorce, I got a call to direct a movie about a marriage that was breaking up. I answered the call.

EXERCISE

1) Write down five occasions when you didn't answer "the call."

2) Express in a paragraph or two the ways and means by which you will be on call in the future.

PRACTICING WITH TAXI DRIVERS

A new position opens up in a prestigious firm and the CEO says, "So what have you been doing?" and the account executive mumbles, "Uh . . . Huh? Well I . . . I did the . . . uh . . . well, I . . . I guess I'm okay. . . ." He freezes. In auditions, casting directors, producers, directors, and agents put actors on the spot. They say, "Tell me a little bit about yourself. . . ." The actor squirms. "I, uh . . . want to . . . really to . . . get this role. . . ." He or she chokes. These authority figures become the omnipotent possessors of the key to life, the be-all and end-all of your career. You give them too much significance. This kind of thinking brings you to a terrifying choke. Is this choking a way of life with you?

As a director I practiced my communication skills with New York taxi drivers to help me solve important and risky problems I had with actors and producers. The risk was if I asked the producer for more money that was needed for a set or costumes, he might blow up and not give it to me. With actors, I was inhibited in asking them to execute some creative idea that I thought was wild. They might balk. Perhaps my communication skills would not be enough. I found myself stuck, inhibited by the fear of dealing with my co-workers. An idea for a game came to me: Try out my persuasive abilities on the New York cabbies. Of course, this might be a bit trickier today—there are a diversity of languages that would create an additional challenge.

If you say to a New York taxi driver, "Take me to 159 Fifth Avenue and wait for me—I'll be down in about four or five minutes," you'll get a look that's unbelievable. Cabbies in New York don't like to wait, because when the cab is not moving the meter runs at a lower rate. So my game was to get in the cab, give the driver a place to go, check out his mood, deal with that mood, and get him on my side so that, by easy request, he would happily wait. I kept practicing until I felt comfortable about this mutually profitable arrangement. I always tipped well.

The routine goes like this: "Hey, how you doing? How long you been driving a cab? Fifteen years! Wow! Say listen, I got a big problem. I don't know what to do."

The driver would say, "Yeah? What's your problem?"

I'd say, "I got this damn '49 De Soto . . ."

He'd say, "I used to drive a De Soto, I loved it. A lot of the cabs used to be De Sotos. What's your problem?"

"Well, it's twenty-two years old. I got transmission trouble."

"I could've told you that. Those friggin' things always got tranny problems."

"You know anybody who can fix the damn things?"

"Sure, sure. My cousin, Bruno, over in Brooklyn.

Works on 'em still. He's got one of his own."

"Convertible?"

"No."

"Mine's convertible."

"Really, buddy! You got a drop top?"

"Yep. All original."

"Wow. That's beautiful."

"So listen, I've got to go up here to 159. Can you wait for me a couple minutes?"

"Hey, no problem. I'll write Bruno's number on this card."

I'm upstairs, downstairs, and on my way in ten minutes. No problem. Why so easy? The De Soto. We had a mutual interest. Common ground. We established an agreeable rapport that superseded the outlandish request of waiting for me.

There is no guarantee that you will always get what you want, but having practiced this approach many times, especially with taxi drivers, it is certainly easier for me to confront the producer with something I need, or ask the actor for a difficult turn I want him to try. Practice this technique in your everyday life when a problem arises—with the grocer, the mechanic, the hairstylist. Find a common interest you can both talk about. Get friendly. Then discuss what you need. This practice, which should become a natural part of your life, will lead you to better results when you're trying to resolve matters in a high-pressure personal or professional situation.

By the way, if you need a great De Soto mechanic, I still have Bruno's hot phone number in Brooklyn.

EXERCISE

1) Name the three people you have the most difficulty communicating with.

2) Name another five on whom you can practice your communication skills. Practice this technique.

3) See if that practice helps you with the original three difficult ones.

HERE COMES TROUBLE

A very accomplished actress with whom I have worked had what I consider to be a most serious problem that held her back from more success: bitterness. She was unhappy with the business and complained about how she had been treated. She engaged in what I call "commissary talk." This is what occurs when a film is being shot and the actors at lunch in the commissary sit around blaming and bitching about the director, producer, and writers. This "commissary talk" often continues even when they are not shooting, and it affects the way they deal with their jobs. And it affects their self-esteem, because when you blame you go right into a hamal attitude—that of people having power over little you. I designed this improvisation, performed with other professional actors at a career seminar I held. The purpose was to let this actress vent her feelings and express her problems and disappointments.

(BEGINNING OF IMPROVISATION)

(ACTRESS enters her AGENT's office.)

ACTRESS: I asked for this meeting. I have been the laying hen for this agency from the moment I arrived in this town. I have brought a lot of money into this company. I am a distinguished actress. I have starred on Broadway, as well as in a television series. All right? Four years on a network series and you never showed up once to ask if I'm okay. Your commission checks came in every week, but I never saw anyone. I am tired of being jammed into the pigeonhole of a comedy actress. I won an Emmy for a dramatic role. I haven't gotten one audition for a dramatic part since then. Have you even seen some of the work I've done? Do you look at my film? Do you?

AGENT: Sure. Of course I've seen you. Yes.

ACTRESS: Then you're one of the few from this agency that has. I want to know why it is that half the young casting agents in this town don't have a clue about what I've done. I was up for a role and they said, "No, no. We're looking for a theater actress." I've been a featured actress on Broadway at least ten times.

AGENT: Honey, you know how the business is today.

ACTRESS: What does that mean?

AGENT: It's the way the business is today.

ACTRESS: What is this bullshit? What does that mean?

AGENT: You're casting me in the role of the standard agent. I'm not. I'm on your side.

ACTRESS: I know you're on my side. You get paid to be.

AGENT: Look . . .

ACTRESS: *(Rising anger.)* What is it that you do?

AGENT: What's going on here? You've always been such a nice person. In four years, you've never once told me any of this.

ACTRESS: I like to be a nice person, but I'm changing.

AGENT: This is bullshit that you're giving me.

ACTRESS: *(Coldly.)* I beg your pardon.

AGENT: Yeah. Bullshit.

ACTRESS: *(Ice.)* I beg your pardon.

AGENT: No, no. You may not beg my pardon. All I hear you saying is: "There are lots of other agents out there." If that's how you feel, then go. Go!

ACTRESS: I see. If that's how it is, that's what I'm going to do, honey.

AGENT: Terrific. Go. Take your poodle and go.

ACTRESS: I don't have a poodle. Before I go I want to talk to the bosses. Shall we talk to them?

AGENT: Talk! Talk to them. Bring the whole damn agency in.

ACTRESS: Okay. But it may mean your job.

AGENT: And what if it means your walking out that door and nobody cares?

ACTRESS: Then I'll know that I'm in the wrong place. And that's all I need to know. Good-bye, sir.

AGENT: Good-bye.

(END OF IMPROVISATION)

MILTON: Okay. Very good. Both of you. Now, you don't feel quite right, do you?

ACTRESS: No.

MILTON: You see, from my point of view, what the agent did was too easy for him and your leaving was too easy for you. This stuff about "you fire me, I fire you" is for the birds. You haven't gotten to all the issues yet. You're still being motivated by your bitterness. It is interfering with your ability to really get at the truth of what you want. Anger and blowing out of the office solves nothing. You wanted to bring the bosses in, so bring them in.

ACTRESS: *(Hesitantly.)* Okay.

MILTON: Well, bring them in.

ACTRESS: The film and television department heads? The bosses?

MILTON: Yes. Now the agent may be accurate. You never spoke about this in four years? People do this. Actors do it. People in many professions do it. They sit on their concerns. They wait four years, like you. Is that true of you? Was it four years?

ACTRESS: Yes.

MILTON: All I'm advocating is, if you're having a fight, a real disagreement with someone, don't let it sit. Clear it up. Maybe it's a pleasant conversation in a restaurant. Maybe it's a letter. Maybe it's the sweetest damn gift he ever saw. A cream puff. Yes, a cream puff to the so-called enemy. It's a "cream puff concept." You feel some real hostility? Send a cream puff. So I don't know what it takes. Maybe two cream puffs. Whatever it takes to get off the hostility and get the real issues resolved. Remember, your agent, your co-worker, can be a gatekeeper for your career, your life, and your future. And maybe even become a dear friend. Let's go on.

(Two actors who portray HEAD OF FILM and HEAD OF TELEVISION come onstage.)

(IMPROVISATION RESTARTS)

AGENT: So you wanted the bosses, they're here. Talk to them.

FILM HEAD: *(Gently to the ACTRESS.)* Look how beautiful you look.

ACTRESS: Come on. Don't bullshit me.

FILM HEAD: *(Handing her a script.)* This is the script I wanted you to look at.

ACTRESS: I said don't bullshit me. Don't try to butter me up. We just had a rotten fight.

AGENT: I'm very upset about this.

ACTRESS: *(To FILM HEAD.)* Don't look at your watch.

TV HEAD: Let her talk. Let her talk.

ACTRESS: I have no problems about what I do. It's what I want to do that I have problems with. I've been on a series for four years. I have made my choice by doing television. I've made a lot of money, I'm very appreciative of that. But the bottom line is for four years no one from this agency ever came near me.

TV HEAD: That's not true. I sent you baskets.

ACTRESS: Never did.

TV HEAD: Well, then, it was my secretary's fault. 'Cause I know every year when that show renews I send you baskets. Beautiful fruit baskets.

FILM HEAD: Please. Let me. *(To ACTRESS.)* I am so glad that we're having this talk. This is what it's all about. This is terrific. This is great.

ACTRESS: I understand this agency has so many clients that you have to rent the Coliseum for your Christmas party. Naturally, you don't have enough time for me anymore.

TV HEAD: That's not true. *(Glaring at AGENT.)* If he doesn't have time for his clients, that's his problem, not the agency's.

AGENT: I'm having a very bad month, both at home and the office. I'm arguing with friends. I can't believe it. Please, I'm arguing with my dearest friends.

ACTRESS: I don't believe the way you treated me was as a friend.

AGENT: You're right. I apologize.

TV HEAD: So, that takes care of that. I've got a four o'clock so I'll just—

ACTRESS: Oh, no you don't. I want to know from all of you what you plan to do to further my career. Okay?

FILM HEAD: Yeah. I have a bit of a problem.

ACTRESS: What is that?

FILM HEAD: I've never had any disinterest in you. So I feel, all of the sudden, like I am being blamed for the whole four years. I feel terrible. I'm very upset.

ACTRESS: (Blowing up.) Oh, no you don't. Don't try to turn the tables on me.

FILM HEAD: I'm not turning. I'm very upset. I've been very loyal to you. Very loyal.

ACTRESS: I'm not talking about loyalty. I'm talking about . . .

(They all talk simultaneously. Bedlam.)

FILM HEAD: Goddamn it. I've had four meetings
like this this week!

TV HEAD: I'm going to walk out this door right
now.

FILM HEAD: Walk out the door. All of you walk
out. I'm tired of people blaming me. I
told her not to take that series, and I
was right.

ACTRESS: That was yesterday. I have no way to
change that. I merely want to know
what will happen now. Convince me
that you believe in me, that you'll do
everything in your power to further my
career, then I'll stay. But I don't want
to be a number on your list.

AGENT: So let's get some ideas. Give us some
ideas.

ACTRESS: There's that Paramount project about
farm people.

AGENT: Oh, we met a little resistance on that.

ACTRESS: From the casting agent?

FILM HEAD: A little resistance.

ACTRESS: You can't go over her head?

FILM HEAD: The director wants someone else and is willing to hold off the picture until he gets her.

ACTRESS: *(Emphatically.)* Well, then, tell me that! Don't let me sit around for weeks calling and saying, "What about getting me in?"

AGENT: You seemed . . . fragile.

ACTRESS: Fragile? There's nothing fragile about me. *(A moment of silence.)* I don't want to make trouble. I am full of talent. It is bursting to come out. I don't want to do the little comedy roles anymore. I've done that. I need your help. I need to know that I have a team behind me that will find every possible avenue to get me in. That's all I want. I want the opportunity to compete. I

don't want trouble. *(To TV HEAD.)*
And I don't need the baskets, honey.

(END OF IMPROVISATION)

MILTON: Good. Do you feel you got it off your chest? You feel better?

ACTRESS: Yes.

MILTON: Good. Now apply this, and talk to the actual guys. By the way, your last line was a little hostile. Let 'em send the baskets. But much better.

This improvisation encompasses much of what I've discussed so far in this book. Blame. Getting Along. Flinch. Hamal. Scarcity. Habit. Choices. Problems. All of these issues are alive in a situation where so much is at stake. We all have to become experts in each area in order to more skillfully get what we want.

One of the really bad habits we have is when we're upset at someone, we tell someone else. This does nothing but fuel our discontent. If A has a problem with B, don't tell C about it. Telling C is a flinch. Tell B—then you have a shot at change.

Don't sit on things. Your family, friends, and co-workers need to know how you feel. The longer you don't express yourself, the longer you don't go after what you need, and the more you pretend everything's fine, the more you'll have built yourself a house of cards for a life. In confronting difficult situations, this house may fall. That's okay, at least then you'll know the truth of where you stand. Now, in its place, you're able to build—with a solid foundation—real relationships to support you and your career.

EXERCISE

1) Review two meetings that you had, business and personal, in which you remember you didn't handle it so well. Note what you could have done to improve those meetings.

2) Secure two meetings (again, business and personal) with people with whom you have to handle a situation.

SHOCK ABSORBERS

Do you believe as I do that friendships need shock absorbers? Cushions? Something to handle the rough road? You're going to have bumps in a friendship, so you better have shock absorbers. These are cushionlike agreements that allow you to avoid blowouts. So when it starts getting rocky in friendships, you're able to cushion the blows and stay on course.

It's the same with a career. You need heavy-duty, factory-installed shock absorbers if you're going to make a successful trip. If there is a disagreement between you and your partner, be interested in the other's viewpoint, and before demanding that yours is heard, shut up and listen. That's a durable shock absorber. If you sense a distance between you and your partner, a pulling away, a coldness, have agreements to reach out for a meeting, a lunch, a talk. That's a durable shock absorber. Or, when you're about to end the relationship, use the Rolls-Royce of shock absorbers—double check and ensure you haven't entered the distorted clouds of Blame Heaven.

Some time ago, after many years of bitterness and rivalry, my two brothers and I met alone in Denver. There were no parents, no friends, no wives, no one. Incredible as it may sound, for the first time in our lives, it was just three mature men alone. I don't mean to overdo this point, but the fact that we had never been alone together, three brothers, with no one else, was a startling revelation to us. This meeting was an effort to bridge the rifts between us. The eldest brother, and perhaps the wisest, set up a shock absorber right up front: no recriminations. No dwelling obsessively on the past. This was a great help. We certainly went at each other and got many issues off our chests. But we didn't get stuck in the past.

One realization we had was that by the three of us never having been alone together, we had protected ourselves from some kind of personal intimacy. Now we seemed to revel in this personal contact and con- centrated on making specific agreements for the future. We wanted a change. We wanted a different relationship. That meeting and our life since with one another has not been without bumps, but the ride is much smoother than it ever was before, and the bumps are in the low register on the Richter scale. Now we get along. We actually have become friends.

As an interesting sidebar to all this, I realized as I was writing this chapter that our meeting, our connect- ing, was itself a major shock absorber in our relation- ship. Without meeting again, we were running the risk of returning to our old ways—out of communication and filling in the blanks with all kinds of accusations and wild scenarios. The fact is we had not met since Denver, so I immediately called both and set up a time, despite our busy schedules, to meet again. We did.

The great cinematographer Charles Lang told me that when he worked on films in France, key members of the crew shook hands every morning on the set, regardless of what had happened the day before. What a shock absorber! One of the best. They knew there were going to be bumps, so they built in a safety net. When I worked with Charles, we made sure to employ the handshake in the French style. Actually, on one occasion, I had to demand that he give me his hand. He did, finally, and we laughed.

This idea of shock absorbers is also needed within oneself. Sometimes you get more than a bump, you get a crash. Almost every director and actor I know who's worth his or her salt has been fired at least once. That's a crash. The death of a loved one. That's a devastating crash. At times like these, when you are wracked with doubt and grief, by all that is held holy, you need top-flight, platinum-plated, depth-retrieving, bounce-back shock absorbers.

Once upon a time, a while ago, I was smashed by a heavy-duty crash. It felt as if a Mack truck had fallen on me. So I applied one of the most simple but effective shock absorbers: Get out of town. That's a good one. It's a good one if you're not merely running away. In my case it was an escape to rehabilitation in Palm Springs. I exercised, trained, swam, played basketball, bicycled, and walked in the sun for a few weeks. As my health was restored and my attitude improved, I reviewed prior successes. I pondered future projects.

At the end of my sojourn, no question, I felt better. I felt ready to rejoin the fight. At these crisis times, what you're trying to do is resurrect belief in yourself, belief in your talent, belief in your future.

EXERCISE

Note down three different relationships you have, business or personal, and devise shock absorbers for each. Use them.

HITCH UP TO YOUR DREAM AGAIN

If your career is stuck in any way, it could be because you're bound up in the defeats and difficulties you may currently be experiencing. So you've tried to do something again and again, and you feel beaten. Let's say you had a notion to open up an art gallery. At first you couldn't find a space, then someone backed out of a contract, then the city didn't give you a building permit, and then the earthquake hit, your dog died, and Aunt Tilly required in-home care. You got tied up in the minutiae of life. The routine of the "you don't always get what you want" world beat you.

Remember, the dream is in essence spiritual and is often defeated by the inexorable machinations of the real world. Of course, you must persist through these obstacles. But here's a tip: Restate your original purpose. Reconnect with the passion you had in the past when you started. If you don't have a career concept, create one. Now. Quick. If you made one in the past, rediscover what your desires were then. Some people claim they are too tired and defeated to look back. Don't buy into that. Look. See what you originally wanted. That's how you refire your dreams and hopes. Dig into your heart, into your desires. You had an original purpose, an original concept. Just simply hitch up to your dream again.

EXERCISE

List some goals you had that you never accomplished. Do you still want to achieve them? What do you need to do to refire these dreams?

CERTAIN DOWN-HOME HINTS

Some certain people always kvetch about other certain people. These certain people always have problems and arguments with other certain people in the business. They break up with them. They avoid them. They don't talk to them again. Certain people always think other certain people think ill of them. These certain people had an argument with these hatefuls and they hate forever. And *ba-da-bum, ba-da-bum, ba-da-bum*—the beat goes on in its spiteful way.

Get out of the "I hate everybody, everybody hates me" rut. Help your career. Try this. You have problems with people? People have problems with you? Make a list of every one of them. If you're an actor, there's the producer you didn't get along with or the director who chose another actor over you. If you're not an actor, make your equivalent list. Anybody, no matter how far back. Go over the list again and again until you make sure you get them all. And then proceed to handle each and every one of them. Resolve your past difficulty by writing each a letter, having lunch, or visiting them. This includes family and friends.

When you meet or write, don't talk about the problem that occurred. Don't tell them how right you were, or how right they were. Just tell them how well you're doing, how happy you are. Tell them something of interest in your life—a new job, a baby on the way, your new apartment. Positive things.

One actress said to me, "I don't think anybody in the business thinks I can act." I said, "Who?" She said, "Everybody." I said, "Who's everybody?" Once she made the list, it was only twelve people. Then, looking at that group, she discovered that just five people actually questioned her talent. This was her "everybody." She communicated to them and resolved the situation with each. Her career started happening.

I've given this assignment many times, and always there's been success to some degree. If there's no positive change in your career, in your life, you missed somebody on the list. Catch them all, and then just watch what good things happen. It's damn effective. Most who do the assignment get the magic thing—work. Some simply feel better. Some have significant career boosts.

Sometimes the first letter you send doesn't work. Then write two or three letters so they know you mean business, and that you're no longer functioning off of mutual negativity. Remember, don't bring up the problem. Just fix things. I've had people go so far as to write these letters to the dead to clear up situations that still haunt them. I've suggested they don't mail them, but definitely write them. Because even the dead can bury us.

Getting over this bump between you and others is very easy to do. Fun, by the way. Joshua Logan, the famous director, told me once, "In this business, never hold a grudge." His advice was straight to the point, a down-home and eminently practical hint for all businesses and for all of life. Try it.

EXERCISE

1) List all the people against whom you're holding a grudge, or who you think are holding something against you.

2) Reach out to each as described above, and watch the results.

WORKING WITH MASTERS

Like it or not, you're in the apprentice system. Although it may not be common knowledge, the apprentice system is still alive in this world. You have to find a way to get certain people into your career. Whether your goal is to be a mechanic, a chef, a tailor, an architect, a trial lawyer, or what have you, there is a master you need to hook up with. I tell my students that all of them at one time or another should be a gofer for their most respected producer or director. Go for their coffee. Go for their lunch. Get close to them. Get in there. Watch them work. This is not just advice for the young. You may need to shake yourself up. You may need to cultivate new, exciting ways out of the routines of your job. No matter the rank to which you've risen in whatever field you're in, to learn a new skill or add nuances to an old one you need to learn from a master—either through observation, participation, or formal study. The Europeans do it all the time. The apprentice system.

Joshua Logan. I wanted to work with him. I was a young, unknown director in New York and I couldn't get to him. I was home on a rainy afternoon, Central Park West. After reading the *Times* and seeing that Mr. Logan was directing a new play, I remembered that he had written the preface to Stanislavski's

Building a Character. Josh had gone to Russia in 1932 to study with the master Stanislavski. I went immediately to the library, looked up the passenger registry for the boat that he sailed on, went back home, and wrote him a note.

Dear Mr. Logan,

1932. October 15. 12:10 P.M. Pier 43. A young director left America to study in Russia with a master. 1957. November 2. 2:30 P.M. Central Park West. This young director wants to study with a master.

Respectfully,
Milton Katselas

Within forty-eight hours the phone rang and a voice said, "Report to Schumer's Warehouse at ten o'clock Monday morning." Monday morning a black Mercedes limo pulled up and Joshua Logan emerged wearing a long fur coat, looking remarkably like Stanislavski. He greeted me and welcomed me to the start of rehearsals for a new play he was directing, *Blue Denim,* written by another master I met at that time, James Leo Herlihy. So I got this wonderful job, working with a master. Josh and I remained friends until his death.

Elia Kazan. I waited for him in the street. I saw him. I approached him. He's Greek, I'm Greek. I spoke to him in Greek. Bingo. I not only worked for him, but we're friends to this day.

Sanford Meisner. He was holding auditions for *The Time of Your Life,* which he was directing at City Center. I wanted to play the newspaper boy. He was Greek. I was Greek. Simple. At my audition, Mr. Meisner asked, "Do you sing like an Irish tenor?" I said, "I'm Greek." He said, "Sing a little." I did. He listened, seemed to be quite startled, and said, "This Greek newspaper boy is supposed to sing like an Irish tenor. Thanks, but not this time." Without missing a beat I asked about the assistant director's job. He said, "No, I already have an assistant." I said fine and graciously left. The day of the first rehearsal I surreptitiously appeared at City Center and walked upstairs and said, "I'm Mr. Meisner's assistant." They ushered me in, and I sat to watch the rehearsal. Mr. Meisner came in, saw me, and asked, "Who are you?" I said, "I'm the Greek who doesn't sing like an Irish tenor." He said, "I already told you, I've got an assistant." I said nothing. He looked at me. I looked at him. He looked away. I looked away. He shrugged and walked away. A few days later the same routine. "What are you doing here?" I said nothing. He shrugged. I shrugged. He walked away. I stayed and watched the whole production unfold. He eventually got to like me slightly.

Lee Strasberg. I approached him in front of the Variety Arts on Forty-sixth Street and asked, "Can I come sit in on a class? I'm in college and I want to observe a class." He said, "No." And I said, "I'm a friend of Mary Morris." She was with the Group Theater, and my teacher at university. Lee said sternly, "She is not our friend." I followed him into the studio and sat down in the back. I looked at him. He looked at me. I looked away. He looked away. He shrugged. I shrugged. He started teaching. I stayed. I studied with Lee, and he was always respectful and nice to me. I was a good student in the private classes, and later directed some scenes at the Actors Studio, where he was most supportive. At one point, Lee said I could come to any class he was teaching. I often took him up on this.

These great directors and teachers were not my only mentors. There was also Tassos, a shoemaker on Columbus Avenue, who was a great influence on me during the lean years. There was Stanley, a gambler in the poolroom I ran for my father—he, too, was a mentor. There was Bernardo for music. James Leo for many things. I selected all of them. The desire and the need is what brings the master. So look around in the pockets of your life. They may be there. Cultivate them. Want them. Need them. Select your masters from all areas of life, not just the area of your profession.

That's my way, and not necessarily yours. I've supported my career by associating with these glorious masters. They helped me with music, writing, relationships. Tassos, the shoemaker, as he hammered away at his work, made me laugh about my plight, because in those tough times he would ask me, "Spaghetti or steak?" to shorthand if I was working or not. Humor, when I so sorely needed it. A master can guide you through his or her talents or experiences to help you with life in general or some more specific skill. Then you can learn to be a master and pass it on. And so it goes.

EXERCISE

1) Find three masters you're already associated with, and figure ways to further these relationships.

2) Find three new masters. Let this list grow as you do.

GIVE

Love has to do with giving. And it is that love expressed that is a key to your career and life. This may sound a little spiritual, but this action is also what makes the ball game go. Caring and giving is how you release your talent, your ability.

Hostility holds you back. It is the wall that prevents you from expressing yourself. Not expressing yourself is hostile, whether your silence is born of anger or meekness. As strange as it may sound, shyness is hostile. Showing up for the job but not participating is hostile. Your justifications are hostile, no matter what the reason is for why you couldn't do something. All of this hostility acts as a cocoon around you. Like a butterfly, shed this cocoon in order to break out and fly.

Has someone ever died before you had a chance to tell him or her what you felt? Have you withheld communication until it was too late? I had a situation once with Sal Mineo. We were rehearsing Jimmy Kirkwood's play *P.S. Your Cat Is Dead* for a Los Angeles production. Eight months earlier I had not chosen him for the role the first time I did the play in San Francisco. After that successful run, we came back to do it in Los Angeles, and this time I picked Sal. So we were rehearsing, and he was wonderful in the part. I turned to him one day and decided to give him what I thought he deserved. I said,

"I've got to tell you something. As good as the other actor was in San Francisco, and he was really good, I still made a mistake in not taking you the first time. This is your part." And he wept. We hugged. Three days later he was dead. I'm so glad I told him.

So with your agents, your bosses, your loved ones, your friends, your partners: Give, baby, give. Let them know what you feel. Let it flow. Now is the time. Don't wait. As my friend the brilliant actress and down-to-earth philosopher Doris Roberts said to me once when I was hesitating about whether or not to go to Europe, "This is not a dress rehearsal, honey." I went.

What better way to build trust with people who are important to you than to speak up and say how you feel? Tell them now. Let it out. Hug them and tell them they're terrific, or show them how, in some way, they can do better, which is another expression of love. If you wait, it may be too late.

EXERCISE

1) State three situations where you're being hostile, and how that hostility is being demonstrated.

2) Pick three people who you need to give to, and do so.

Unlikely Winners

Jimmy Durante	Dustin Hoffman
Danny DeVito	Humphrey Bogart
Helen Keller	Stevie Wonder
Roseanne	Barbra Streisand
Dudley Moore	Lily Tomlin
Whoopi Goldberg	Anton Chekhov
Arnold Schwarzenegger	Little Richard
Bette Midler	Woody Allen
Linda Hunt	Christie Brown
Ronald Reagan	Robert DeNiro
Elia Kazan	Ray Charles
Oprah Winfrey	Henri de Toulouse-Lautrec
Abraham Lincoln	Dr. Ruth
Nelson Mandela	Colin Powell
Carol Burnett	Frederick Douglass
Janet Reno	Spud Webb (5'6" NBA player)
Jackie Mason	Jimmy Carter
Mahatma Gandhi	Billie Holiday
Robert Redford	Julia Roberts

Unlikely winners all. If you closely examine each person on this list, society could easily have a prejudice about them. These unlikely winners could be considered, by certain conventional standards, to have a flaw, a serious career problem. It's something they've had to overcome.

At one time, Picasso, Sartre, and Charlie Chaplin met. One of them was heard to say, "Three tiny men." The tallest was five foot six. You may ask why I included the handsome Robert Redford and beautiful Julia Roberts. Because in this society there is not only a prejudice against unattractiveness but also one that says if you're beautiful, talent may not be close by.

Who's a likely winner, anyhow? I don't know. All winners are unlikely. Yet everybody has a chance in this horse race if they can go beyond what others may consider their handicap, their eccentricity, their inappropriateness. Two men quite dissimilar in nature spoke at my classes. First Cary Grant said, "All you have is you." Then Marty Ritt, the film director, said, "Mine the vein of gold within you." It's the hardest thing to nail, but you and your uniqueness is all the winner there is.

EXERCISE

1) State three ways in which the world would consider you an unlikely winner.

2) State three ways you consider that you're unique.

A FREEWHEELING DISCUSSION

On Negativity, Despondency, Victimhood, Eating It, Vigilance, Your Family, Blame, Moving the Pebble, Priorities, Persistence, Solutions, Flinch, Ethics, and Survival.

J: Handling my mother's will and estate is a real problem. Why am I the one who has to handle it? It's always me. I just want to move on, but I feel there are at least five more years of rage and grief I have to explore.

MILTON: Move on. By all means. But get off the complaint that you're the one who has to handle the will. You probably are the most suited to do it. So do it. But most important, why are you exploring five more years of grief? Who says you've got to carry these years of rage and grief with you?

J: I just feel overwhelmed by it all.

MILTON: I understand. But who says you've got five years of this crap? See? That's the decision that's burying you.

J: But it feels like I do.

MILTON: You're strongly contributing to that
                feeling. Mourn her, yes, but don't
                keep exploring and dredging up your
                feelings.

J: So if I made the decision, I can drop it.

MILTON: Yep. Why do you need to go through
                five years of abject misery? Who needs
                that? Listen, most of what happens to
                any of us is based on our own deci-
                sions. You made a decision, and if
                you're not careful, you'll get it coming
                at you in full bloom. It's hard to cop to,
                but that's the truth. Be careful what
                you wish for—you might get it. By the
                way, five more years of guilt and suf-
                fering? God! This is what sucks up
                your energy. This hang-up with your
                mother's estate is just the apparent
                problem. Get to the real problem and
                deal with that. The real problem has to
                do with you. What is it?

J: Oh, God. I just worry about this career
                sometimes.

MILTON: Right. Your career is where this energy should go. Get off your moaning and groaning thing. You need to focus and put your energy into the career. When you've done this in the past, you've done well. So do again what was successful. Yes? You had a question?

R: Sometimes I just feel so down.

MILTON: Sounds just like the last question. Is there a happy person in the room? Despondency with a young person is, you know, absolutely absurd. Especially an attractive young person such as yourself. How can you be convincingly despondent? You'll have to whiten your hair, get a cane, walk all bent over. Then it might be believable. What do you have to be despondent about? Your life is just beginning.

R: I'm not despondent.

MILTON: You said you felt down. What is this? Cheeriness?

R: I'm thinking.

MILTON: Okay. But ask yourself something: "Why am I thinking despondently?" Why, if you're thinking about all these heavy career matters, aren't you saying, "Jesus, I'd better get going!" Like those guys in the forties musicals: *(Singing.)* "Better get going! Better get moving! Gotta go! Gotta go! Gotta go!!!" Has anybody been telling you that your career is in the dumper?

R: Well, yeah. They always tell you that.

MILTON: They do?!! Who's they?

R: People around me. Family.

MILTON: Oh, great. Family. You have any high heels?

R: Yeah.

MILTON: Do these relatives have feet?

R: Yeah.

MILTON: *(Acts out stamping heel on foot à la flamenco dance.)* Ahhhhhhh! You better do something about it. Because I tell you this is a real hard business. Very difficult. Support comes from the Latin *portare,* "to carry." To lift you. To be fully behind you. And if you don't have the support of the people around you, you've got no chance! You've no chance because every time you accomplish something, this somebody else negates it.

R: Do I just stomp them with the stilettos right away?

MILTON: They don't have to be given the heel on the big toe the first time around. If they're friends or family, talk to them. If they're business associates, talk to them.

R: They keep giving me statistics of what a low percentage there is of working actors.

MILTON: Right.

R: I feel like I just want to say, "Shut up, already. I'm susceptible to this negativity and criticism. Don't tell me about how impossible an acting career is."

MILTON: That's right, tell them. Go on.

R: Go on?

MILTON: With what you were saying. Tell them. Tell them what you want to say.

R: Okay. "Don't tell me if this doesn't work out you'll give me a job at the plant. I don't want a job at the plant. I want to be an artist and you have to help me. If you love me, you will. If you don't, help me anyhow."

MILTON: Good. Now you have to tell the real people.

R: Really? You mean actually talk to them?

MILTON: Yeah. I've done it in my life and it isn't always pretty. But it isn't as difficult as we imagine. After many meetings, having tried all you can, you may have to get tough.

R: Like, "Listen. You love me? Don't sabotage me anymore."

MILTON: Yeah. And then add, "You do this crit-
           icism, this put-down, this negativity
           once more and you won't see me
           again." Usually on the spot they
           straighten out. Because they love you.
           They'll say, "We do love you. We'll
           support you."

R: I don't know if I can talk to them.

MILTON: You gotta find out where you stand
           with these people.

R: I'll try.

MILTON: Don't try. Do it. Talk to them three or
           four times, and then sharpen your heels.

R: Okay.

MILTON: Someone else?

V: Shall I just go after one dream at a time?
           I'm an actress, but I'm also a singer.

MILTON: What's your priority?

V: I don't know.

MILTON: Look, I'll be ostracized for saying it, but if you must have a marriage and a mistress, so be it. But you can't have two marriages. I've taught a lot of people over the years who have this hyphenate thing: photographer-actor, singer-actor, actor-model-photographer-singer. Great. It's all wonderful. Celebrate the abundance. But set your priorities. It's okay if they change in three weeks. Now, if you shift twenty times a year, you've got a problem. Simply set your priority, then it's just a matter of administration. So if you must have both a wife and a mistress— and God knows it doesn't even work in Italy—allocate your time very, very carefully. Yes?

L: Let's say that you're in an addictive situation. I'm in recovery now and I've had a lot of problems with my family, so they're not so supportive of what I'm doing because of my past track record. How do I turn that around? I'm working a twelve-step program and doing what I have to do for me, yet I don't have that support from my family.

MILTON: This support thing keeps coming up. Interesting. Who is it in particular?

L: My father. I don't feel strong enough to talk to him.

MILTON: I got you. You're doing the twelve steps. Tremendous courage. You've got to be some kind of woman to stay on that. Don't flinch now. What would you say to your father about your progress?

L: I'd say, "I'm sober, I'm in a twelve-step program, and I'm winning. I'm getting stronger every day."

MILTON: I like it so far. What else?

L: "I'm doing the hard part. I'm getting my life in hand. Got anything to say about that?"

MILTON: Very good. Seems to me you're in a position to talk to your dad right now. What do you think?

L: It's tough. . . .

MILTON: Yes, I know.

L: Well, I guess I can do it. . . .

MILTON: Good. Anybody else?

F: You know, it's like I'm walking around and telling off everybody in the world except the person I need to speak to. It's like the feeling of being righteously angry with my friends is more fun than simply dealing with what's up.

MILTON: Yeah. To be righteously angry with anybody is for the birds.

F: Absolutely.

MILTON: All you want to do is pick up the pebble and move it with the least amount of effort. Like you said, deal with what's up. It's simple. Just pick up the pebble and move it. You don't need self-righteousness, you don't need blame, you don't need anger. There's something to get done. Just do it. Just move the pebble. Who's next? I feel like a short-order cook.

B: Suppose you can't contact the agent you want to speak with?

MILTON: What? This guy's dead, or what?

B: No, I can't get past the secretary.

MILTON: Oh, there are other ways to do it. You wait for him in the parking lot. You find out where he has lunch. You write him a letter. You send him a cake.

B: And if he doesn't respond?

MILTON: Send him another one.

B: Should I go to another agent?

MILTON: No. Did you send the one you want a cake?

B: No. They don't like my cakes.

MILTON: Come on, you didn't send any cake.

B: I can't even bake.

MILTON: Don't fool around. Send him a cake. He doesn't respond? Send him champagne. He doesn't respond? Send him a girl. He doesn't respond? Send him a guy. Do what you've got to do. And then when you've really done it, you can say, "Hey, I've done what I can." Then go to the next agent. But you haven't even sent one cake. I know the feeling. You call, don't get through, and you say, "To hell with him." That's too easy. Try again. Be tenacious. Maybe he doesn't like cakes. Send him a big casaba melon. Uncut, so he knows there's no bomb inside. Be resourceful. Just don't give up. Anybody else?

Y: Why can't I seem to get a better place to live?

MILTON: This is, you know . . . You guys think I'm the Answer Man or something. I'm not the Answer Man. I just ask questions, trying to provoke the truth for each individual. Each of you has to find the truth for yourself, then I add my two cents to the equation in an effort to edge you toward your own understanding. Anyway. A better place to live. All right. One of my students lived in a certain neighborhood, and I said, "You've got to get out of there." It was the worst. Finally I said, "How can you live in a place like that?" What do you think the reason was?

Y: Because he was used to it.

MILTON: That's right.

Y: Yeah. Habit, right?

MILTON: That's right. Go on.

Y: He needs to change the habit.

MILTON: That's right. What else? What does he need to do?

Y: He needs to make more . . .

MILTON: Yeah. More what? Say it.

Y: More money, more money.

MILTON: There. You said it. How?

Y: I don't know.

MILTON: C'mon.

Y: I deserve more. . . .

MILTON: That's for sure. Check your self-esteem.

Y: God, my place is really horrible.

MILTON: If you demand it, and get yourself better stuff . . .

Y: I know, I know, I'll feel better. I know.

MILTON: Your demand for better starts with your own self-esteem, the feeling that you deserve better. Self-esteem gets you a happier place.

Y: And if I feel better, I can do more?

MILTON: And get more. Invite me to dinner when you move into your new place. Yes?

C: I have a question about flinch. How do you stop doing it?

MILTON: You catch yourself in the act. Flinching. Watch yourself doing it. It's fascinating. The trick of avoidance.

When you see it, and it's not a pretty picture, nail yourself in the act. Stop this slippery weakness. Then do the right thing. Change. Make the call. Write the letter. Talk to your husband. Talk to Mom. Flinch and you get weaker and weaker. Face up and you get stronger.

C: If you catch yourself flinching, you try to complete the job right then and there?

MILTON: Right then and there! Flinch, like doubt, is a disease, possibly terminal. If you don't treat it right away, it festers, gains, and eventually takes over. Life will challenge you. Don't flinch. Eyes wide open and alert. Straight ahead.

EXERCISE

1) Take three situations where you feel stuck, unable to accomplish what you want.

2) Analyze them and discover which chapters from this book apply. Reread those chapters.

3) Apply the information from those chapters to these situations.

CAREER CHECKLIST

_____ Decide that the career I'm in is for me. Really.

_____ Put my career concept down on paper. Simply, clearly, precisely.

_____ Focus my priorities by writing them down. Choose.

_____ Write down where I am now, where I want to be, how I can attain it.

_____ I want a job. Which job? Contact those in a position to help me.

_____ Have a clean, bright, happy place to live.

_____ Get a desk. Exclusively mine. Get a phone. Mine. Create a base of operations.

_____ Log my appointment schedule on paper.

_____ Keep a clear To Do list, and check it off as I complete each item.

_____ Be a pro. Never say, "It can't be done." Do what I have to do to get what I want.

_____ Prepare for big choices by achieving decisive, confidence-building small choices.

_____ Fire up my dream again by restating my original purpose on paper.

____ Write the letters I've been putting off.

____ List my accomplishments. Validation upholds confidence.

____ Contact those who don't think I can do it. Change their minds.

____ Work out a clear, practical personal budget on paper.

____ Form healthy partnerships with my boss and with my business associates.

____ Check my friends and family. Are they supportive? If not, resolve.

____ Ensure that second jobs don't deplete my energy, but provide sufficient financial support.

____ Whatever I'm doing, be there. Awake, alive, seeing something new every moment.

____ Sweep the alley. Do my job. Don't listen to distractions.

____ Stamp out negativity in myself and others.

____ Talk, don't fight. Cooperate.

____ Never hold a grudge.

____ No apology. No pale substitutes for me. Give all I've got.

____ Blame sucks. Others do not do it to me. I do it.

___   I am not a hamal. I am valuable. Act accordingly.

___   Seek the advice of others, weigh their advice, then in the end do it as I see it.

___   Be fully aware of habits. Abolish the bad ones, do more of the good.

___   Read. Put my ear up and let the guy talk into it.

___   Look up words I don't understand. If one definition leads to another, keep looking.

___   Be an "artistic killer." Trying is not enough. Get it done. Totally. No justifications.

___   Don't eat it. Talk up.

___   What's good for my career need not be a family sacrifice. If it is, work it out.

___   Keep the Failure Monster out of the picture. It scares away creativity.

___   Act on the fact that life is happening now. Now. This is not a dress rehearsal.

___   Resolve to be a winner. I may appear to be an unlikely candidate. But it's not so.

___   Maintain a positive, upbeat view of myself. Otherwise, why should others?

___   Don't buy into the idea of scarcity. It's a lie. *Abbondanza!*

____ Confused? Go to the beach. Take a walk. Get away. Make a choice. Come back.

____ Build in emotional shock absorbers for the bumps.

____ Reward my victories, great and small. A nice dinner, a cake, a gift to myself.

____ Exercise physically to cope with the demands of stress.

____ Attend plays, concerts, galleries, sports, movies. Read. Travel. Be a world citizen.

____ Seek out masters. Work with masters. Become a master. Pass it on.

THE DANCE

The most difficult thing to face and deal with is your life. What is it? What do you want it to be? What should it be? What do you do to achieve it? What's acceptable? What's kosher? What's not?

Is life a wild snake that has eaten peyote and is compulsively thrashing about, taking you where it wants to go, frightening you, threatening or actually biting you, coiling around your neck and strangling you, or simply poisoning you until you're dead? Are you following the mesmerizing undulations and dancing to the serpent's tune, unable to do anything as the clock ticks? Is this the way it is? No. It's not true. The snake can be guided, led, seduced, cajoled, and instructed.

Life need not be something we are in awe of, overwhelmed and frightened by. Nor do we need to be continually critical in our approach to life. Awe, fear, and criticism of our own lives, or of others', lead us to a lower self-esteem, a disastrous response. Not a good resolution for life. These ways retard us and relegate us to second banana, supporting player, an extra in some sumptuous Hollywood extravaganza. In truth, it's your movie the whole way. You're the writer, producer, director, and lead actor, and it's all based on your original story and idea.

What you do in the course of your life—your

choices—creates your story line, your journey. It's important what you do, but how you do it is what really counts. That's what it's all about. There is an art to doing whatever you do. There is an art to living. Can you choose? Can you determine? Can you make it go as you wish? Can you decide, then execute? Yes. Yes. Yes.

Life is yours. It can be understood. It can be seen. If it can be seen, it can be won. You are not in a rudderless barge on a rampaging river that just takes you endlessly downstream. It's really possible for you to look the snake square in the eye, transform its poison into a serum, its bite into a kiss, its coiled strangulation into an embrace, its mesmerizing dance into your tango. It's yours. You are the snake. You are the dancer and the dance.

INDEX

A

Abbondanza, 111, 174
Accomplishment,
    personal, 27
Addiction, 72–73
    to failure, 84–85
    and relationships, 73
Angelou, Maya, 106
Anna Karenina, 47
Apathy, 73
Apology, 75
Apprenticeship, 148
Aronson, Boris, 75
Arrogance, 11
Art, personal views on, 27
Artistic killer, 66
Authority figures, 23, 25
    authors as, 44–45
    and blocks to success,
        29–31
Avocations, personal,
    78–83

B

Balance, 54
Beast of burden, 29
Being present, 49-51
Blame, 86–92
    definition of, 88, 89, 90
    discussion encompass-
        ing, 157–71

disempowerment and, 91
exercise for avoiding, 97
external influences as
    object of, 86–87, 94
improvisation encom-
    passing, 126–37
nobility of, 93
Blue Denim, 149
Bly, Robert, 80
Bogart, Humphrey, 112
Boxer, acting like a, 14–15
Braque, Georges, 105–106
Budget, 12
Building a Character, 149
Business, personal views
    on, 27

C

Cab drivers, 122–25
Career
    choice of, 6
    as culmination of
        dreams, 87
    definition of, 6, 7
    flinching and, 61
    growth and, 69
    ship metaphor for, 8
    stuck period in, 65
    Terrorist Theater and,
        65–67
Career checklist, 172–75

Career concept, 10–16
  self-expression and, 15
  writing your, 12–13,
    15–16, 17
Career crisis, 8
Caring, 153
Caution, voices of, 23
Celebration, 68
Change, 69–74
  personal contact lead-
    ing to, 140
  solving problems to,
    137–38
Chaplin Charlie, 156
Cheerfulness, 75
Choice, 19–21
  character traits as, 74
  as a game, 21
  habit as, 71
  improvisation encom-
    passing, 126–37
  life decisions and,
    176–77
  options and, 20
  perfection syndrome
    and, 22–25
  prerequisites for, 49
  review of, 21
Citrano, Lenny, 46–48
Commissary talk, 126
Commitment, 22
Common ground, estab-
  lishing, 124
Communication
  direct, 137–38
  with parents, 31–34

  with people in general,
    53
  positive intention and,
    54, 94–95
  reading as, 40
  relationships and, 26
Communication skills,
    122–25
  establishing common
    ground and, 124
Concept, 10
  detail in, 11
  effect on physical real-
    ity of, 11
  energy and, 13–14
Confidence, 27
  destruction of, 33
  problem solving and,
    107
Conflict, 54
  balance and, 54
  confrontation and, 93
  humor and, 54
  resolution of, 96–97,
    131
Conformation, 53
Confrontation, 25
  role playing and, 31–34,
    126–37
  of a situation, 51
Contact, personal, 140
Cooperation, 55
  exercise to foster, 56
Crawford, Joan, 113
Creative impulses, 53

D

Dance, 176, 177
Day job syndrome, 117
Deadline, 65
Decision, basis of, 20–21
Decorum, 23
Deming, W. Edwards, 105
Demons, internal, 62–64
Denial, of personal feelings, 51
   flinching and, 60
DeNiro, Robert, 15
Despondency, 159
Dictionary, 41
   purchase of, 48
   use of, 46
Doubt, 60
   failure and, 84–85
Dreamer, 2
   definition of, 4
Dreamlike, definition of, 3
Dreams
   aspects of, 4
   choosing your, 70–71
   definition of, 1
   essence of, 143–144
   fear of personal, 7
   money and, 12
   placement of unrealized, 61
   writing your, 9, 10–11
Dyslexia, 42
   as a decision, 42

E

Eating it, 50, 52
   discussion encompassing, 157–71
Emily Lowe Competition, 11
Energy, 80, 159
Ethics, 157
External influence, 62–64
   blaming, for failure, 86–92

F

Failure monster, 84–85, 174
Failure, personal, 29
   seductiveness of, 84–85
Fear, 60
   letting go of, 108–11
Fight, definition of, 54
Flexibility, 49
   growth and, 69
Flinch, 60
   career problems and, 61
   definition of, 60–61
   discussion encompassing, 157–71
   exercise for recognizing, 64
   external influences and, 62–64
   passivity and, 61
   personal demons and, 62–64

Friends, 7, 23, 26, 27, 45,
103, 104, 134, 149,
150, 151, 154, 166
For Whom the Bell Tolls, 47
From Here to Eternity, 47

G

Giving, 153–54
love and, 153
Good moves, 77
Grant, Cary, 24, 156
Growth, personal, 69
and forfeit, 69

H

Habits, 71
daydreaming as, 73
exercise for recogniz-
ing, 74
improvisation encom-
passing, 126–37
Hamal attitude, 37
commissary talk and,
126
Hamal, 29
Hamlet and, 35–39
improvisation encom-
passing, 126–37
reading and the, 47
Hamlet, 37, 38, 39
scene from, 35–36
Hate, 33
as a rut, 145
Hemingway, Ernest, 47
Herlihy, James Leo, 76, 151

Hint, 74, 147
Hostility, 153
Humiliation, 36
Humor, 54

I

Idea, 14
Inner/outer voices, 62-64
Intelligence, reading and,
40–41, 45
Intimacy, personal, 140

J

Jones, James, 47
Justice of the world, 24

K

Kazan, Elia, 53, 104, 149–50
Kazantzakis, 73
King, Martin Luther, Jr., 2
Kirkwood, Jimmy, 153
Krishnamurti, 73

L

Lang, Charles, 141
Launching pad checklist, 18
Law and Order, 8
Levity, 78–83
Lifestyle, chasing a, 117–18
Likability, 53
Listening, 44
Logan, Joshua, 104, 146,
148–49
Love, 153

M

Martyrdom, 70
Masters, working with,
    148–52, 175
Meisner, Sanford, 104, 150
Mineo, Sal, 153
Modesty, 23
Money
    and dreams, 12
    problems blamed on, 103
    self-esteem and, 100
Morris, Mary, 151
Motive, 23
Music, as a hobby, 30

N

Needs, personal, 93
Negative v. positive, evalu-
    ation of, 20
Newman, Paul, 13

O

Observation of the present,
    49
Obstacles, 13–14
Old ways, 27–28
Operating base, 17–18
Opinion, 26
    art and, 27
    business and, 27
    other people's, 27
    race and, 27
    religion and, 27
    sex and, 27
    writing your, 28

Options, 20
Original purpose, 143

P

P.S. Your Cat Is Dead, 153
Painting, 10–11
    personal demons and,
        63
Parental support, 31–34
Passivity, 61, 85
Patience, 36
    and avoiding blame, 96
Peer pressure, avoiding, 63
Perfection syndrome,
        22–25
    choice and, 22
    commitment and, 22
    listing areas of life
        regarding the, 14
    parents and, 25, 32–33, 79
    society and, 23–24
    voices of caution and, 23
Perfectionism, 23
Perseverance, 14
Personal space, 17–18
Personality, importance of
    unique, 27
Physical reality
    concept and, 11
    transformation of
        dreams to, 3–4
Picasso, Pablo, 105, 156
Plan, 10
Point of view, personal, 50
Positive affirmation,
        145–46

Positive intention, 54
  and confronting conflict,
    94–95
Potential, 5
  Terrorist Theater and, 65
Praise, 94–95
Pride, 69
Priorities, 78
Problem solving, 53
  expression of problems
    and, 126
  success and, 105
Propriety, 23
Protest, 94
Psychology, 16
  age of, 13

R

Race, personal views on, 27
Rapport, 124
Reading disabilities, 42–43
Reading, 40
  definition of, 40
  dictionary and, 41, 46, 48
  dyslexia and, 42
  grasping content
    while, 41
  intelligence and,
    40–41, 45
  trauma associated
    with, 41
Relationships
  addiction and, 73
  communication in, 26
  letting go of, 108
  with parents, 25, 31–34

Religion, personal views
  on, 27
Respect, 34
Risk taking, 53
  and Terrorist Theater, 66
Ritt, Marty, 156
Roberts, Doris, 154
Role playing, 31–36, 126–37

S

Scarcity, 108–11
  and fear of losing, 109
  improvisation encom-
    passing, 126–37
Seductiveness, 60
Self-defeat, 87
Self-esteem, 49
  commissary talk and,
    126
  personal entitlement
    and, 98–101
  self-punishment and,
    98–101
Self-expression, 15
  outward affirmation of,
    75–76
Self-indulgence, 120
Self-pity, 75
Self-punishment, 98–101
Sensibility, 23
Sex, personal views on, 27
Shock absorbers, 139–42
Situation, 20
  addressing a, 51
  recognizing problems
    in a, 103

Solution, problem as the,
102–107
Statement of personal
dream, 5
Stern, Joe, 8
Strasberg, Lee, 150–51
Success, 12
Survival, 157

T

Talent, 153
Terrorist Theater, 65–67
deadline in, 65
Time of Your Life, The, 150
Tolstoy, 47
Trauma, personal, 41

U

UCLA, 42
Unconditional love, 34
Unexpected catastrophes,
119–20, 143
Unlikely winners, list of,
155

V

Values, personal, 27
Victimhood
blame and, 88–89
discussion encompass-
ing, 157–71

W

Waiting, 9
Warrior, 80
Work space, 17–18
Worry, 73
Wright, Frank Lloyd, 106
Writing dreams, 9, 10–11

Z

Zorba the Greek, 73

About the cover

This is a monotype, which, simply stated, means one print only of each work of art produced off a press. This print, which was created specifically for *Dreams Into Action,* is then reproduced onto the cover. I love creating monotypes, which I just started to do about two years ago. I work on them in a nice, intimate studio in Santa Monica. It's such fun, with happy friends around, good food and hot salsa music accompanying our every move. *The Dance of Action* is the name of this print, which resonates with the energy needed to move one's career. Please accept this monotype as a statement of the start of many beautiful changes and fulfillments in your life.